SUPERPLONK

Malcolm Gluck writes the Superplonk column in *Weekend Guardian* and a monthly wine column for the Scottish *Sunday Post Magazine*. He is consultant wine editor to Sainsbury's *The Magazine* and wine editor of *Cosmopolitan*. He has also written for *Punch*, *She*, *Country Living*, *Independent on Sunday* and the *Sunday Express*. He often appears on TV and speaks on radio. He is also the author (with Antony Worrall Thompson) of *Supernosh*. He is preparing a book on French hypermarket wine and a travel book on the world's vineyards.

SUPERPLONK

Gluck's Guide to Supermarket Wine

MALCOLM GLUCK

faber and faber
LONDON · BOSTON

First published in 1991
by Faber and Faber Limited
3 Queen Square London WC1N 3AU
Second edition published in 1991
Third edition published in 1992
This new edition first published in 1993

Photoset by Parker Typesetting Service, Leicester
Printed in England by Clays Ltd, St Ives plc

© Malcolm Gluck, 1993

Malcolm Gluck is hereby identified as author of this work in accordance
with Section 77 of the Copyright, Designs and Patents Act 1988

The author and publishers gratefully acknowledge the
Estate of P. G. Wodehouse and Hutchinson Books Ltd
for permission to reprint material (on page 12) from
Meet Mr Mulliner by P. G. Wodehouse.

A CIP record for this book is available from the British Library

ISBN 0 571 16928 7

10 9 8 7 6 5 4 3 2 1

TO IVY
who would have been astounded
AND HARRY
who would have laughed

Contents

Introduction

This must be the first book in Faber's history to have no place on a bookshelf. It fits more comfortably in a car's glove compartment or a shopping bag. It will not yield to being shrunk and squeezed into the Reader's Digest or to having a waiting list compiled for it at the local library. It will be thumbed in the hurly burly of Tesco's or the hubbub of Morrisons – not to mention Asda, Budgen, the Co-op, Gateway, Littlewoods, Marks and Spencer, Safeway, Sainsbury's, Waitrose and, for the first time, Kwik Save (and I would have included the Scottish group William Low but they couldn't get their wine list or their wines to me in time).

These are the heroes and heroines of the book: supermarkets. Those temples of consumerism where wine is just another commodity like cabbages and cornflakes. Those marvellous Texas ranch-sized bungalows where no rabid assistants lurk to bite the incessant browser. The places where the best wine bargains of all can be unearthed.

Supermarkets don't suit the wine collector, the wine snob, or the seeker after the status putatively conferred by grand and hugely overpriced labels. Supermarkets are unpretentious places where wine is bought with one hand trundling a trolley, the other gripping a three-year-old child. (Quite which hand this leaves free to pluck out a bottle of wine let alone leaf through this book is not a question I shall attempt to answer at this time.) Supermarkets' only lack is an impartial adviser on hand to point out the smartest bottles. The little book rectifies this omission.

This is the fourth edition of this book which, like the others, has been completely rewritten from scratch. It is not yet as fat as I am but is is getting there. There is no accident about either enlargement. My engorged tum is due to my drinking my way through zillions of bottles every month, with many of those bottles being matched with various foods, and my swelling tome is due to the increase in the number of bargain bottles worth including. This is heartening news to everyone (even my doctor, who may be unenthusiastic about my increase in weight but is as keen as the next person to hear of the bargains in his local supermarket). Tastier and tastier wines are piling up on the shelves so how can I forbid them entry?

Yet still there are folk, wine-bibbers to the bottom of their boots, walking the streets of Britain who are not only blithely unaware of the many superb supermarket wines but equally ignorant of their low prices. I found myself on Merseyside in the spring, talking to a long-established pop singer who actually said to me: 'You mean, man, you actually recommend people drink wine which costs under a fiver?' He was serious. And though he probably lives in a suede-lined house, sleeps in flared silk pyjamas, and wouldn't know a supermarket trolley if it ran over him, his attitude is not uncommon. A fortnight before I met him, a woman ran up to me in a Midlands supermarket, kissed me on the cheek, and said, 'Thank you for stopping my husband being a wine snob. We've saved a fortune since I bought him your book.' When, moments later, she introduced to me to her husband, a most congenial chap who politely ignored the lipstick I later discovered on my cheek, he told me that until he'd read *Superplonk* he'd never thought of paying under £7 for a bottle of good wine made from the classic grape varieties he enjoys. Now he's cheerfully guzzling bottles some of which, to his continued amazement, cost barely three quid.

The classic grape varieties, like certain chardonnays and

cabernet sauvignons from Australia, a couple of pinot blancs and merlots from Hungary, several sauvignon blancs from New Zealand and one or two from Chile, pinot noirs from California and eastern Europe, have shone as bargain beacons of brilliance this year. The structure of these so-called New World wines has owed much to the traditional wine-growing regions of Europe; yet though they compare well with their more famed counterparts (in some cases even beating them hollow for aroma and fruitiness) these New wines cost a fraction, in some cases a ridiculously insignificant fraction, of the Old ones. This is good news. It's even good news for those traditional wine regions because in some cases they've been forced to rethink their pricing policies and to start work improving their wines.

This trend does, interestingly, follow the hilariously pretentious yet thoroughly researched TINT phenomenon respected by marketing gurus the world over, even though it was conceived as a piece of satire inside an advertising agency twenty years ago. TINT stands for The Imitative Number Two and three famous examples are Pepsi Cola, Avis Rent-a-Car and Penthouse magazine; there are hundreds of others. I will not bore you with the complex mathematical formulae underpinning the success of this marketing theory for the interest here is purely in drinkers being able to buy a Californian pinot noir, say, for under a fiver whereas the wine it is blueprinted from in Burgundy costs thirty and can't offer half as much perky fruit.

Competition and flattering imitation in this manner is always healthy, and inevitable in a business like wine, but it is downright stupid and shortsighted if, seeing the success of a neighbouring TINT vineyard, other growers jump on the bandwagon and promptly fall off in the process. They may fail because they lack either the ingenuity to produce the right quality fruit or the skill to vinify that fruit in order to achieve the desired result. But often the failure is due to the simple unsuitability of their situation, soil and climate, what the French winningly call *le terroir*, to allow the famous variety to flourish. For every one successful inexpensive classic varietal copy, which I applaud, there are a dozen failures. My back teeth are fed up with tasting more and more indifferent, indistinct chardonnays and cabernet sauvignons from obscure areas of the globe.

In following this route, grape varieties better suited to these areas' climates become neglected by the local wine-growers. This is a serious oversight. Chardonnay, for instance, has become a brand almost in the league of Coca-Cola but it's possible to taste a hundred wines made from that variety from a hundred different producers from twenty different countries and never once come across an acceptable commonality of fruit and style: some chardonnays sting you with their acidity, others bruise you with their fruit. And they can each lay legitimate claim to be a chardonnay. This is all right by me if the wine is very drinkable and very cheap like, say, some of the brilliant examples from Australia, but I'm bothered by the Coca-Cola analogy because in the end it's self-defeating unless, like that soft drink, you can guarantee a uniformity of flavour every time and give your consumers no unpleasant surprises. For this reason, I would prefer not to see grape varieties predominant on wine labels. If young winemakers wish to copy their decrepit old masters, why not also follow them down the road of varietal indifference? When did you last see a bottle of burgundy with the words 'pinot noir' on it? Or a claret proclaim itself 'cabernet sauvignon'? The canny French are brilliant marketeers and they know that although a grape variety can be grown anywhere, only two brands in the world can be labelled Burgundy and Bordeaux. Our antipodean cousins are also dab hands at labelling their wines with all sorts of weird and wonderful individual names, as are many Californians, and I much prefer this way of doing things. Cloudy Bay from New Zealand is a shining example of the vineyard predominating over grape variety, though every seasoned drinker knows the grape is sauvignon blanc as they know Le Montrachet is chardonnay, and as a result of this policy Cloudy Bay is rapidly becoming an international brand with all the security that confers.

Fortunately, following anyone else's lead or dog-trotting after fashion is, for some growers, anathema. Therefore although there are genuinely brilliant classic grape varietal bottles from New World areas, as much excitement, I reckon, is with the less well-known and indigenous varieties which are also pouring in from all over the place – eastern Europe, California, South Africa. Wines made from blauer zweigelt from Austria, kekfrancos from Hungary, pinotage from the Cape, zinfandel from the States have all been cheap and cheerful wonders this year. These wines offer more satisfying day-to-day drinking at a cheaper price than do many pricier wines which rely upon the fame of their grape variety to command attention. Along with the wines coming from older wine regions, previously not highly regarded or gaining fresh reputation after years of decline, these are where many attractive bargains are to be found. Let the wine buffs of America and Japan have their hugely overpriced bordeaux and burgundies; let them scorn to touch the more immediately drinkable rustic nobodies from the obscure recesses of the Languedoc and Provence, parts of Spain and southern Italy, not to mention Portugal, Germany and, perhaps most stag-gering of all, dear old Blighty herself. I now happily glug the wines from several English vineyards and they go very well with the humble pie I always feel must be my staple fare on such occasions in penance for the slagging-off I have given these wines in the past.

Nowadays, my focus has changed. I don't think about wine the way I used to. I don't taste wine the way I used to. Likely climate, location, grape variety have been elbowed. I'm not bothered about barrel ageing, it rarely enters my head unless it confers more value to the wine, and I'm unlikely to spare even a tinker's cuss as to whether a winemaker's picked his grapes riper than normal, kept the blessed stuff on its lees, or employed a particular filtering system to finish the wine off (which, of course, unmannered filtering does for good).

Now when I smell, taste and contemplate a wine, I concern myself with one thing and one thing only. Is it good value for money? How does its taste and effect stack up against similar wines and how does it compare in price? I taste a clean white wine, with a measure of melony fruit, and whether it's sauvignon blanc or zoldveltilini, whether it's from New Zealand or Moravia, whether it's £20 the bottle or £2, I sample the wine firmly saddled to my hobby-horse and nothing can unseat me. Indeed, hobby-horse it no longer is; it has become an animal of an altogether more spirited and indelible a disposition – a profession-horse. I rejoice whether I come across a cheap varietal beauty, knocking into a cocked hat its expensive Old World counterpart, or a terrific wine from a vineyard and a grape variety no one's heard of before.

I hope, certainly it is intended, that the readers of this book enjoy the benefits of my equine obsession with value for money. No other wine critic looks at wine this way, or rates wines the way I do, but then no other wine critic devotes the majority of his or her time exclusively to supermarkets and their wines. The effects on my metabolism are a small price to pay for the sheer thrill of finding brilliant, cheap wines.

Can the supermarkets keep it up? They have, after all, been

in the forefront of the wine-drinking revolution in this country for some years and it might be thought, what with several of the big high street wine shops getting their acts together and even some old-school-tie wine merchants screwing up their pride and offering cheap bottles, that some of the super-markets might be feeling the competition. The answer is, yes they can keep it and no, they are not feeling the competition in any way whatsoever. The supermarkets' share of the off-trade business in this country is now approaching three and a half out of every five bottles sold. For them, the clouds of the recession have been silver-lined with newer attitudes among wine drinkers which have developed, to the supermarket's huge advantage, in several ways.

Many drinkers who previously exclusively patronized wine merchants now buy their everyday drinking wines at super-markets because they cannot afford to ignore the bargains: point one. The tide of critical acclaim necessary to bolster the morale of these drinkers, especially those prepared, due to straitened circumstances, to give cheaper New World copies of classic European varietals a chance, has grown immensely over the past two years: point two: The recession has been so vicious and wallet-felt across all classes in society that displays of parsimony are actually fashionable and so many a man – and we are, of course, talking about the male of the species here (for women have never experienced the slightest unease at dumping a wire basket bulging with bargains on a super-market checkout counter) – has acquired a new comfort in allowing inexpensive bottles on his dinner-party table labelled J. Bloggs Supermarkets plc when as recently as two years ago he would have gone naked and unshaven on the 8.15 to Waterloo rather than sanction such a public statement of provenance: point three.

Supermarket wine, then, has added respectability and

acceptability to its previous acknowledged charms of avail-
ability and accessibility. Only the glamour is missing. Or is it?
Last summer, supermarkets became sexy for the first time
ever. Oxbridge undergraduates considered including 'Supermarketing' on their list of preferred spheres of work to rank
alongside 'Publishing' and 'BBC-TV programme research'
as popular careerist fantasies. Japanese tourists were demanding to be taken around the larger of our temples of consumerism as they are escorted around St Paul's Cathedral. It
was Sainsbury's who created this new image when, anxious to
prove that the eponymous family were not the only relations at
work in the company, two enterprising employees practised
the carnal variety in a busy non-smoking standard class car-
riage of British Rail to the complete indifference of the other
passengers only to cause outrage and protest, and thereby to
become celebrities, when the pair lit up cigarettes during a
brief respite in their steamy lovemaking. Hitting back, Tesco
immediately signed up James Major, son of John and Norma,
to work at one of their Cambridgeshire branches during his
summer vacation.

Such brilliant PR coups, however, will never, I'm pleased
to say, crush the spirit of local wine merchants who really
know their onions and offer a wide range of decent wines
from around the world. If they can't compete with the local
supermarkets on price, or glamorous employees, they can
surely knock spots off them when it comes to giving impartial
advice and turning up on customers' doorsteps with urgent
deliveries. And many a specialist wine merchant, with a large
and unrivalled range from carefully chosen vineyards from
just one country and smaller ranges from two or three others,
is a joy. But for the scruffy local off-licence flogging overpriced rubbish, the writing is on the wall. And what of the
future for the fancy wine merchant with his over-priced

classics, his inflated ego, and a dependence on an uncritically rich ovine clientele happy to be herded from one famous vineyard area to another? Once can only guess that they are slowly going the way of their customers: one of whom is forever lost every time an up-market newspaper publishes an obituary citing likely cause of death as cirrhosis.

The future for supermarket wine, then, is red, white and rosé. As long as my own liver, as one considerate correspondent hoped, keeps tickety-boo, I shall continue to slug it out. Cheers!

How this guide works

Each supermarket in this guide is separately listed in alphabetical order. Each has its own introduction with the wines logically arranged by country of origin, red and white (including rosés). Each wine's name is as printed on its label.

Each wine is rated on points out of 20. In practice, wines scoring fewer than 10 points are not included although sometimes, because a particular bottle has really got my goat and scored so miserably I feel readers might be amused by its inclusion, I stick in a low pointer. Over the past five years, you may be interested to know, this miserable vinous underclass has assaulted my palate in steadily decreasing numbers.

An excellent supermarket wine can be so characterized because of its price, not only because it is rewarding to drink. I have made it unmistakably clear in my introduction to this book how much value for money is taken on board when I rate a wine. I expect expensive wines to be good but I do not always expect good wines to be expensive. Thus, a brilliant £10 bottle may not offer better value than a £3 wine because, although the pricier wine is more impressive it is not, in my eyes, anywhere near three times as impressive.

The full scoring system, from my initial tasting and

scoring point of view, works as follows:

20 Is outstanding and faultless in all departments: smell, taste and finish in the throat. Worth the price, even if you have to take out a second mortgage.

19 A superb wine. Almost perfect.

18 An excellent wine but lacking the depth and sublime finesse for the top. Extremely good value.

17 An exciting, well-made wine at an affordable price.

16 Very good wine indeed. Good enough for *any* dinner party. Not expensive.

15 For the money, a great mouthful with real style.

14 The top end of everyday drinking wine. Well-made and to be seriously recommended at the price.

13 Good wine, not badly made. Not great, but very drinkable.

12 Everyday drinking wine at a sensible price.

11 Drinkable, but not a wine to dwell on.

10 Average wine (at a low price), yet still a passable mouthful. Also, wines which are expensive and, though drinkable, do not justify their high price.

9 Cheap plonk. Acceptable for parties in dustbin-sized dispensers.

8 On the rough side. Chemicals showing through.

7 Good for pickling onions.

6 Hardly drinkable except by desperate drinkers on an icy night by a raging bonfire.

5 Wine with all its defects and mass manufacturing methods showing.

4 Not good at any price.

3 A palate polluter and barely drinkable.

2 Rat poison. Not to be recommended to anyone, even winos.

1 Beyond the pale. Awful. Even Lucretia Borgia wouldn't serve it.

For easy reference a condensed version of these ratings is to be found on the very last page of the book.

Prices

I cannot guarantee the price of any wine in this guide for all the usual trite reasons: inflation, economic conditions overseas, the narrow margins on some supermarket wines making it difficult to maintain consistent prices for very long and, of course, the existence of those freebooters at the Exchequer who are liable to up taxes which the supermarkets cannot help but pass on to the consumer. To get around this problem a price banding code is assigned to each wine:

A Under £2.50   B £2.50–3.50   C £3.50–5
D £5–7   E £7–10   F £10–13
G £13–20   H Over £20

Acknowledgements

I work alone, but I cannot survive without the help, advice and encouragement of others and so I thank my two Faber editors, Sarah Gleadell and Belinda Matthews, for their support. I also feel blessed by the enthusiasm of this publisher's publicity, sales, production and design departments, not to mention those terrific booksellers (and they know who they are) who sell so many copies of this book. I am in debt to *Weekend Guardian*, its courageous editor and saintly Food & Drink editor, and all those of its readers who have written to me over the past year. I thank Fiona Lindsay and Linda Shanks for their unstinting zeal, as I do the PR departments and wine buyers of all the supermarkets who have been so helpful to me.

Asda

It is arguable whether travel broadens the mind but it seems unquestionably to broaden the grape. Wine gains something from a long sea voyage (as Raj bibbers discovered when their liquid rations arrived from Blighty) and this something it is uniquely given to the British to appreciate. Lacking a commercially impressive indigenous wine industry about which we can yet feel properly chauvinistic, though it is improving all the time, we think nothing of guzzling wines grown 12,000 miles away and many of these wines have been immeasurably improved by their journeys to these shores.

The arid volume doubtless being written at this moment by some humourless British wine scholar on the effects of sea crossings on wine is bound to acknowledge its debt to the wine buyers at Asda. For Asda's wine buyers feel the call of the sea most keenly. The store's Chilean sauvignon blanc, for example, has not been allowed to cross the equator on its tod as do other sauvignons from this part of the world. Asda buyers felt a judicious amount of semillon was needed to give the sauvignon more breadth; to give the wine, in the buyers' own words, 'extra body to enable it to ride out the long sea journey'. Without that semillon and that journey we should not, perhaps, be able to enjoy such florally fragrant and firmly fruity yet clean finishing wine, rating 15 points, for under three quid. In the same way, Asda's sparkling wine, Australian Pinot Noir Chardonnay Brut is also an exceptional 14-point wine which its travels have done much to shape and improve. As blended for the journey from Australia, the wine was, the Asda buyer responsible told me, deliberately made 'austere and steely' so that the wine would mature to such an extent that the bottles on the shelves would offer only soft and friendly bubbles. And so they do. The wine has a delicious introductory aroma of melon and peardrops which is carried through, most attractively, to the fruit. Maybe there's a lesson here for English winemakers: it's not enough to press the grapes, you also need to pressgang the bottles and send them across the equator.

The store insists 'It 'as to be Asda', but this feeble stab at being contemporary and street-credible has not, I am glad to say, affected the wine department. The two gentlemen running it are the epitome of old-fashioned courtesy and charm who would no more drop an aitch than an umlaut (unlike yours truly) and they have, appositely, some charming old-fashioned wines.

Indeed, how Phil and Nick manage with only two noses between them when Safeway and Sainsbury's, for example, have departments with at least eight noses apiece baffles me. I have nothing but admiration for so many bottles in their range. Other supermarket wine buyers I could mention, but won't, feel the same way (and also feel as mystified as I am as to how the two of them do it).

There is no doubt that Asda has worked hard to keep costs at a minimum although this has not affected the number of weird and wonderful wine labels the store expensively invests in. And it is an investment. The only pity is that all that emphasis on design in the store, both in product-labelling and the whole atmospheric way the store is laid out, passes the vast majority of consumers by because the public face of the store most non-customers see, through its advertising, does not do the store justice. It's no good blaming the recession for this. Tesco has trail-blazed with lovable Dagenham Dud in its longer TV commercials, to be matched by Sainsbury's which (via an advertising agency which must, I can only assume, be a fan of Delia Smith and her magic dishes) put recipes into commercials, effectively and compellingly, for the first time. But where was Asda with all this going on? Here's a store which has invested millions of pounds in the most thrillingly modern layouts of any supermarket, matched by labels streets ahead of anyone else's for originality and pizzazz, and first they told us 'It 'as to be Asda' and now they tell us nothing.

Come on, Asda. Tell your ad agency to pull its finger out and join the last decade of the twentieth century. Tell them to go shopping in the store. Order them to take their children there. Insist they drink the wines. Surely, you can get them to drink the *wines*, can't you?

You could always send the ignorant perishers copies of this book.

ARGENTINIAN WINE – *red*

Trapiche Cabernet Sauvignon 1990   13   £B
Give it just a few more months in the bottle and – wham!

AUSTRALIAN WINE – *red*

Berri Estates Cabernet Sauvignon/Shiraz 1990   14   £C
Terrific value – made to spice up a beef stew (whether you drink it or cook with it).

Hardys Nottage Hill Cabernet Sauvignon 1991   15   £C
Brilliant value. Teeth-coatingly rich and delicious fruit of elegance and power.

McWilliams Hillside Shiraz/Cabernet   14   £E

**McWilliams Mount Pleasant Cabernet/Merlot
1989**   12   £C

Oxford Landing Cabernet/Shiraz 1989   13   £C

South Australia Cabernet Sauvignon 1989   15   £C
A distinct mint attack on the nose as you dip into it and then
lashings of keen plummy, cherry, blackcurrant fruit hits the
tongue. Excellent stuff.

South Australia Cabernet Sauvignon 1990   14   £C
So soft and fruity on the tongue it's like liquid toffee.
Delicious.

South Australia Shiraz 1990   13   £C
Not as striking as some and the fruit, though attractive, has a
pastille quality to it.

South Eastern Australia Shiraz/Cabernet 1990   14   £B
Cheering liquid composed of dry plums, sweet cherries and a
very subtle touch of green peppercorn. Quite amazing value.

South Eastern Australia Shiraz/Cabernet 1991   14   £B
Masses of silky finished smoky plum fruit.

AUSTRALIAN WINE – *white*

Goundrey Estate Langton Chardonnay 1992   16   £C
This Goundrey chardonnay creates the most serendipitously
magical a marriage between a plate of fish and chips and a
bottle of wine it is possible to imagine. Has so much exemp-
lary fruit (lychee, pineapple, melon – all subtle, mind, not

aggressive and tinned-fruity) and elegant balance, it's embarrassing – especially to any European chardonnay costing over a tenner. It's an utterly compelling Australian wine and if, as Tristram Shandy said, it is 'more pardonable to trespass against truth than beauty' then I should give it 20 because it was, in the circumstances in which it was drunk (with fried haddock and chips), flawlessly beautiful tippling.

Hardys R.R. 1992   11   £C
The R.R. can only stand for Robert Redford, for this handsomely packaged wine is definitely for old, sweet-toothed drinkers. In truth, R.R. is a marketing exercise which attempts to create a wine for drinkers looking to break out of the grip of liebfraumilch. Having myself broken out of this grip by the age of eight, I cannot say this wine held great charms for me personally. But I would certainly offer it to Aunt Augusta if she were still alive and mewing.

Hill Smith Old Triangle Riesling 1991   13   £C
A most acceptable aperitif but it is as like a riesling as parsley and buttercup posset.

Hunter Estate Chardonnay 1990   12   £D

McWilliams Mount Pleasant Semillon/
Chardonnay   13 ('88)   £C
                                                       12 ('90)   £C

Mitchelton Marsanne 1992   13   £C

Oxford Landing Chardonnay 1990   13   £C

South Australia Chardonnay 1990   14   £C
Oleaginous buttery fruit counterpointed by pineappley acid. Good with grilled chicken dishes. A marvellous lunatic label.

South Australia Chardonnay 1991 16 £C
I love this butter-rich tapestry of rich fruit threaded into which are golden seams of citric acidity. Delicious. Great with grilled chicken and duck.

South-Eastern Australian Semillon/Chardonnay 1992 14 £B
Mustn't grumble at this price – and it isn't as heavy with elephantine fruit as some, but nimble-footed and well-laced acidically. Great aperitif and great value.

BULGARIAN WINE – *red*

Merlot 1988 12 £B

CHILEAN WINE – *red*

Cabernet Merlot (Asda) 14 £B
Handsome youngster with, surprisingly, a full beard of hairy fruit. Roast food wine.

Montes Cabernet Sauvignon 1989 14 £C
Delicious, elegant stuff for any dinner table.

Rowanbrook Cabernet Malbec 1992 14 £B
Good depth of fruit. Well-made wine. Very good value.

CHILEAN WINE – *white and rosé*

Santa Helena Chilean Rosé 1992   15   £B
   Helena and I went on the Heath
   With a tuna fish salad sarnie.
   I found an oak to lie beneath
   And all was bliss, no blarney.

   An alfresco feast unfolded there
   With this cherry bright fruity wine.
   My happy world had no care
   And all I'd spent was £2.89.

Sauvignon Blanc 1992 (Asda)   15   £B
Ooh! What delicious fruit here – like squashy melon and
bananas – but undercut and freshened by good vibrant acidity.
Great structure.

ENGLISH WINE – *white*

Tenterden Cinque Port Classic 1989   14   £C
Underrated, under £4, and selling like cold cakes. Pity.

FRENCH WINE – *red*

Beaujolais (Asda)   12   £B
Cheap and cheerful.

Beaujolais-Villages, Domaine des Ronze 1990   13   £C
A very decent price for a decently meaty wine. And there
aren't many beaujolais you can say that about these days.

Cabernet Sauvignon Vin de Pays d'Oc   14   £B
Typical baked clay dryness of the grape but not the austerity
which this sometimes implies. Lovely soft fruit with buried
flavours. Great with roast meat. Under three quid, this is
some bottle: rich and captivatingly blackcurranty, and pos-
sessed of considerable style.

Cahors (Asda)   12   £B

Caramany Côtes du Roussillon Villages 1990   13   £C
A nondescript bouquet but thereafter some sound soft fruit.
Good price. Also available in a charming magnum.

Château de Cabriac, Corbières 1989 and
1990   16 ('89)   £D
                                              14 ('90)   £D
The '89 is one of the best bargains on any supermarket shelf,
with its aroma of berries, leaves and gently charred wood,
deep rich flavour and firm finish. The '90 is coming along.

Château de Parenchère, Bordeaux Supérieur   14   £C
Improving fast in bottle and in time for this Christmas, I
fancy.

Château du Bois de la Garde, Côtes du Rhône   13   £C

Château Hanteillan, Haut-Médoc 1989   13   £D

Château Haut-Saric, Bordeaux 1990   13   £B
This is a well-made wine, a true claret, and the price is plainly
daft.

Château La Vergne Moulin, Bordeaux 1990   14   £B
Classic furry fruit of the blend (merlot, cabernet sauvignon
and cabernet franc). Delicious with roast lamb etc.

**Château Mayne de Grissac, Côtes de Bourg
1990   13   £C**
Rather a spiky little wine which needs to soften considerably
to be comfortable on the tongue. Lay down for next year?

Château Val-Joanis, Côtes du Luberon 1990   15   £C
Under four quid but punching in the six-quid middle-weight
Côtes du Rhône league.

Château Vieux Georget 1989   12   £C

Châteauneuf-du-Pape, Château Fines Riches   13   £D

Claret (Asda)   12   £B

Côtes du Rhône, Domaine de la Ramière 1991   14   £C
Not much to smell but a lot to savour with its soft and subtly
earthy raspberry and plum and blackberry fruit.

Domaine Bunan Cabernet Sauvignon   12   £C

Domaine de Barjac, Vin de Pays du Gard 1990   12   £B

**Domaine de Grangeneuve, Côteaux du
Tricastin   13   £C**

Domaine de St-Laurent, Vin de Pays d'Hérault 13   £B

Fitou (Asda)   13   £B
Dry, earthy, pleasant fruit: excellent value bottle.

Fronton, Côtes Frontonnais 1989 (Asda)   11   £B

Merlot, Vin de Pays d'Oc (Asda) 14 £B
Ripe, dry, slightly spicy (green pepper) yet soft. A highly approachable bottle.

Morgon, Michel Jambon 1990 13 £D
Some meat on the fruit here. Typical Morgon in style.

Red Burgundy 1989 (Asda) 11 £C

St-Chinian (Asda) 13 £B
Light and fruity and good value.

St-Emilion (Asda) 13 £C

Santenay, Foulot, Château Perruchot 1988 12 £E

Syrah, Vin de Pays des Collines Rhodaniennes 13 £C

Vin de Pays des Bouches du Rhône (Asda) 12 £B

Vin de Pays des Côtes de Gascogne 12 £C

Volnay, Domaine Henri Boillot 1986 13 £E
This is a wine of some weight which included a price tag of £12-odd in the 1993 edition but by late summer this had gone down to just over £8. Asda customers doing the sensible thing, it seems.

FRENCH WINE – *white*

Blanc de Blancs (Asda) 11 £A

Burgundy 1990 (Asda) 11 £C

Chablis 1991 (Asda) 12 £D

Chablis Grand Cru Bougros 1988 12 £G

Chablis Premier Cru Fourchaume 1989   13   £E

Chardonnay, Vin de Pays d'Oc (Asda)   12   £C

Château Filhot 1985 (half)   15   £D
A perfectly splendid wine for the Christmas pudding or
whenever you feel like drowning yourself in honey.

Château Fondarzac Entre-Deux-Mers 1992   15   £C
Outstanding melony, pineappley mouthful. Quite delicious
and good value. Excellent with fish dishes.

**Chenin, Vin de Pays de la Haute Vallée de
l'Aude**   14   £B
An excellently balanced wine of some character. Great value.
Very modern in style, clean and fresh. Don't go near muscadet when you can pick up quality like this at so much less.

Côtes de Duras   13   £B
Most attractive and excellent value: good fruit, good acid, and
not a bad bone in its body.

Domaine de la Tuilerie Grenache Blanc 1991   14   £C
A vin de pays d'Oc made by peripatetic prestidigitator Hugh
Ryman, who manages to conjure an extraordinary level and
intensity of fruit from a funny old grape: talcum-powdery,
melony, a touch of cherry, and is there a smidgen of
gooseberry in there?

**Domaine de St-Laurent, Vin de Pays de
l'Hérault**   13   £B
Good level of fruit, rather dusty aroma, but good value for
large gatherings.

Fortant Sauvignon Blanc 1992   15   £C
Has the keen, refreshing feel of the grape but it also has some
bright sunny fruit of some finesse. One of those wines which,

opened among friends, causes instant delighted comment or,
served to a member of the opposite sex towards whom one has
amorous intent, creates immediate lip-smacking pleasure.
Sadly, a designer person from the winery has crawled all over
the bottle and instead of the winemaker being named and
congratulated we are offered instead the name of a contemporary artist called Jean-Pierre Formica.

Gewürztraminer 1990 (Asda) 12 £D

Mâcon-Vire, Domaine des Chazelles 1990 12 £D

Muscadet, Domaine Gautron 1990 13 £C
From the best area of the region which typically produces a
fuller and more satisfying muscadet. For the money, this is one
of the more attractive of its kind on sale.

Muscadet Sur Lie, Domaine Guy Bossard 1992 14 £C
A muscadet with fruit! This hasn't happened since 1948. A
cause for celebration (and to buy this organic wine).

Muscat Cuvée Henry Peyrottes 15 £B
'The effect is instant and gratifying. As I drained my first glass,
it seemed to me that a torchlight procession, of whose existence
I had hitherto not been aware, had begun to march down my
throat and explore the recesses of my stomach. The second
glass, though slightly too heavily charged with molten lava, was
extremely palatable. It helped the torchlight procession along
by adding to it a brass band of singular sweetness of tone. And
with the third somebody began to touch off fireworks in my
head.' Thank you, Sir Pelham Grenville Wodehouse.

Muscat de Rivesaltes, Domaine de Canterane 15 £C
A honey nougat wine, with apricot and crème brûlée overtones,
which offers a beautiful finish of tangy marmalade.

Pinot Blanc (Asda)   13   £C

Pouilly-Fumé, Domaine Patrick Coulbois 1989   12   £E
Pleasant enough: green-edged and nut-fruity.

Rully, Domaine du Chapitre 1988   11   £E

Sancerre, Domaine de la Porte du Caillou 1991   13   £E

Vin de Pays des Côtes de Gascogne   14   £B
A superbly fruity and generous wine. Lush style. Very
attractive.

Vouvray, Domaine de l'Epinay 1990   12   £D
Good aperitif.

GERMAN WINE – *white*

Baden Dry (Asda)   12   £B

Bereich Bernkastel (Asda)   11   £B

Flonheimer Adelberg 1990   15   £B
Ridiculous price. Has lovely grass and spring flower smells
along with delicious well-developed fruit which some weight
to the finish. Get home from work (hell) and open a bottle
(heaven).

Graacher Himmelreich Riesling Kabinett   15   £D
Brilliant value aperitif. As invigorating to the tastebuds as a
fresh spring day to the soul.

Herxheimer Himmelreich Huxelrebe (half)   15   £E
Like putting your nose into forbidden fruit – exotic, spicy,

sweet and soul-destroying. Flowery, pungent, acidic – cellared for five years it'll be even lovelier.

Mainzer Domherr Spätlese 1992 (Asda)   13   £B
Excellent value. Full of balanced fruit and acid.

Niersteiner Rosenberg Riesling Kabinett   13   £C

Niersteiner Spiegelberg Kabinett 1992 (Asda)   13   £B
Brilliant little bargain.

Rudesheimer Rosengarten (Asda)   11   £B

Wachenheimer Rechbachel 1988   16   £D
One of those uniquely Rhine wines which fairly rattles the molars with gloriously searing sherbet-lemon fruit after first offering the delicate fragrancy of lime zest and spring flowers. Has improved enormously in bottle over the past two years.

Wehlener Sonnenuhr Riesling Kabinett 1990   12   £D

**Wiltinger Braunfels Riesling Kabinett,
Von Volxem**   13   £C
Brilliant but raw. Keep for ten years and have a 17-point wine.

Wiltinger Scharzberg 1989   11   £B

HUNGARIAN WINE – *red*

Cabernet Sauvignon Villany 1992   12   £B

Kekfrancos Villany 1992   14   £B
Go for the soft almond spicy plum fruit. Pizza wine.

Merlot Villany   12   £B

HUNGARIAN WINE – *white*

Chardonnay Dunavar	11 £B

Chardonnay Mecsekaljou 1992   13   £B
Decent firmness of fruit which is a touch sweet to finish.

Gyöngyös Estate Sauvignon Blanc 1991   15   £B
I've tasted Hungarian sauvignon blanc as old as 1947 (in
1993) but I wouldn't advise the faint-hearted to attempt a
glass. This '91 wine has been made to be drunk young and so
won't improve in bottle much, but even so this one is holding
up well (and there are a few bottles still on shelf).

Muscat Dunavar 1992   14   £B
Superb spicy melon aperitif.

Pinot Blanc Dunavar 1992   12   £B

Tokay Aszu, 3 Puttonyos Schlumberger 1981   14   £D
You either like a pud wine which tastes like sour orange
marmalade with a sherry-like undertone or you don't. It's an
acquired taste, to be sure, and an expensive one.

ITALIAN WINE – *red*

Barbera d'Asti Cantine Gemma 1990   15   £C
Baked apple and curranty undertones to the ripe fruit which
offers violets, plums and an overall splendid sense of balance.

Bardolino (Asda)   12   £B

Carbone, Aglianico del Vulture 1987 16 £C
The Carbone brothers make it from the aglianico grape in the
province of Basilicata and the Vulture bit refers to the local
volcano of that name and it is this inhospitable bedrock which
gives the wine its distinctive character. This 13% wine has
faint echoes of liquorice (rather like a barolo), a rich fruit with
a very subtle marzipan or almond touch to it, and it rounds off
this remarkable recipe with a medicinal finish, thick and
linctus-like, which is deliciously compelling. It is a real thinking drinkers' wine with its mineral quirkiness and sturdy
individuality and it is splendid stuff. Don't serve to your
honey-throated mother-in-law unless you want her to choke
to death.

Chianti 1991 (Asda) 13 £B

Chianti Classico 1990 (Asda) 13 £C

Chianti Salvanza Colli Senesi 1991 14 £B
Delicious, plummy, light style with subtle terracotta touches
to the fruit which are typical of the area.

Ciro Rosso Classico 1990 13 £C

Montepulciano d'Abruzzo, Miglianico 1990 15 £B
Cheap and cheering. The earthiness of the dry cherries is
delicious with herby and garlicky roasts and pastas.

Rosso Conero Umani Ronchi 1990 14 £B
Soft and cuddly and full of supple, well-textured fruit.

Rosso di Montalcino, Val di Suga 1990 13 £C

Sangiovese delle Marche 13 £B

ITALIAN WINE – *white*

Bianco di Custoza, Zenato 1989   13 £C
Delicious but perilously close to a fiver.

Chardonnay di Alto Adige (Asda)   13 £C

Est! Est! Est!!! 1990   13 £C
If only more wines had names like this. There's one hugely
overpriced Italian I'd love to see renamed Naf! Naff! Nafff!!!

Frascati (Asda)   11 £B

Lugana Santa Christina 1990   14 £D
Elegance, breeziness, brightness.

Orvieto Classico Cardeto 1992   13 £B

Pinot Grigio di Alto Adige 1992   13 £C
Lots of tongue-lashingly voluptuous fruit.

Verdicchio delle Marche (Asda)   13 £B
Excellent soft fruit and clean acidity. Good value and great
with fish.

Vino da Tavola Bianco   14 £B
White table wine certainly sounds a more romantic proposition in the Italian language and this example can sit on
swankier tables than most. Has melons and lemons chiming
together most harmoniously.

PORTUGUESE WINE – *red*

Barraida   15   £B
Typical dry, rich fruit, figgy and full.

Dāo 1988   15   £B
Dark cherries, plums and currants. No, not a Christmas
pudding but the predominant fruit flavours in this terrific
tipple. Vigorous, well-fleshed out, it makes delicious drinking
for what amounts to little more than a pittance.

Douro 1991 (Asda)   13   £B

10-year-old Tawny Port (Asda)   14   £D
Try it with Christmas cake. Brilliant!

PORTUGUESE WINE – *white*

Douro 1990 and 91 (Asda)   13   £B
Excellent value under £3.

Vinho Verde   13   £B

ROMANIAN WINE – *red*

Feteasca/Cabernet Sauvignon   15   £B
I'm a great fan of this combination of the local grape and the
big international star. When they're on song this pair is as
fruity and mellifluous, as husky and harmonious, and as old-
fashioned in tone as a Crosby and Sinatra duet.

Romanian Pinot Noir 1986   13   £B
Won't somebody take pity on this one? It's been hanging
around Asda's shelves for the devil of a long time.

SOUTH AFRICAN WINE – *red*

Clearsprings Cape   13   £B
Can't argue with the value for money aspect of this wine.

Fairview Estate Shiraz 1990   13   £C
Take your medicine like a heroine! Looks like a spicy bottle of
quack muscle enlarger but it only coats the tongue like one.
Love it. (Or hate it.) Needs a culinary challenge like a juniper-
stuffed and roasted pork chop smothered in Gentleman's
Relish and piri-piri sauce to bring out the best in it.

Landskroom Pinotage 1990   12   £C

SOUTH AFRICAN WINE – *white*

Clearsprings Cape   13   £B
Dry but with lots of ripe melon and plummy fruit and a rather
sweet fruit finish. Good price.

Danie de Wet Rhine Riesling Reserve 1991   15   £C
A hell of a good stab at producing one of those beautifully
balanced aristocratic German wines for which our forefathers,
in the last century, paid more per case than they did for Château
Lafite. Rich, ripe fruit, steely acid, this is an excellently

priced aperitif wine. The '92 vintage, which will also be
available when this book is, I have been unable to taste yet.

Van Louveren Chardonnay 1990	12	£D

Van Louveren Sauvignon Blanc 1993   14 £C
Pineapple and peardrops. Very attractive proposition for
grilled fish.

SPANISH WINE – *red*

**Montecillo 'Viña Monty' Rioja Gran Reserva
1985**   10 £D
Right old fart with knock-kneed fruit. But some people think
this sort of mature thing marvellous (including some distinguished and mature wine writers).

Don Darias   14 £B
Exuberantly flows the Don.

Navarra (Asda)   13 £B

Rioja 1987 (Asda)   15 £B
A truly inviting wine (much improved in bottle over the year)
of vanilla and bananas; not in heavy-handed, riotous form but
rather elegant, and the fresh acid balance pulls it all together
to make a memorable bottle. A bargain light rioja.

Torres Coronas 1989   13 £C

Valencia Red   11 £B

Vega Cubillas Ribero del Duero 1986   13 £C
You can find some funny, and interesting, old Spaniards
hanging around Asda's shelves.

Viña Albali, Valdepeñas 1986   14   £B
Could easily transform a stuffed festival fowl into a feast.

SPANISH WINE – *white*

Fino Sherry Quinta Osborne y Cía   15   £D
Bone-dry perfection. Salty, clean and superb.

La Mancha 1991 (Asda)   13   £A

Moscatel de Valencia   15   £B
One of the best-value pud plonks on the planet.

Valencia Dry (Asda)   13   £A
Great value. Clean, citric, bright with fruit.

USA WINE – *red*

Columbia Pinot Noir 1988   14   £D
A most engaging wine. I used to dream about the '87.

Sebastiani Merlot   13   £C
Delicious, soft fruit.

USA WINE – *white*

Bel Arbors Chardonnay 1991   12   £C

Bel Arbors Sauvignon Blanc 1990   14 £C
Refined, delicious, well-balanced, good fruit, firm acid – a
thoroughly satisfying performer.

Sebastiani Chardonnay   13 £C
Heavy, oily, woody quality of considerable appeal to chicken
and fish stew eaters.

SPARKLING WINE/CHAMPAGNE

Asti Spumante (Asda)   14 £C
Great mango and apricot custard of a wine for pouring over
your tongue with pudding.

Australian Pinot noir/Chardonnay   14 £D

Ayala Château d'Ay 1985   10 £G

Cava (Asda)   14 £C
Soft, earthy, delicious. Very stylish.

Champagne Brut (Asda)   12 £F

Champagne de Venoge, Blanc de Noirs   15 £G
Marvellous fizz fronted by a marvellous phiz; for the wine is as
distinguished, quaint and old-fashioned as the handlebar-
moustached Saki character on the label – and as individual. A
superb oaty, toasty, elegant, and long-finishing bubbly.

Champagne Rosé Brut (Asda)   14 £F

Edmond Mazure Vintage Brut 1989   14 £D
Buttered digestive biscuits. Rich, classy and distinctive. The
past year in bottle has vivified the fruit no end.

River Run Export Brut Reserve, Australia   14   £C
Under four-fifty for a sparkling wine suggests some corners
have been cut, but who gives a damn if the wine is such decent
peachy stuff as this is – with even, dare I say, a touch of
elegance to it. An excellent fizzer for the dosh.

Scharffenberger Brut, California   15   £E
A rich, flavourful fizzer of considerable class. A beautifully
made product. For those times when you feel that vintage
Bollinger is not quite up to it.

Budgen

'P.S. What is a Budgen?' was the parting riposte of a northern *Guardian* reader in his letter to me and I was able to reply that it was nothing to worry his head about. But southern wine drinkers, especially those living in inner-city areas, know exactly what a Budgen is and, if they're smart, they will also know that the wine department is fast improving.

The store has opened newer and brighter stores and introduced friendlier and better planned areas for its wines. The New World wine range, red and white, is interesting (you don't, for example, see the curious Californian grape variety charbono in many supermarket wines but Budgen has a bottle) and there are several bargain bottles from the old-established wine regions of Europe. Although it caters for many customers whose palates do not travel beyond lieb-fraumilch or lambrusco, Budgen also have, in some cases in only a few strategically placed branches, excellent bottles which any wine shop would be pleased to carry. The store has one of the best Côtes de Gascogne whites (Tuilerie du Bosc 1991), one of Italy's most elegant whites (Lugana Villa Flora 1991), a decent cheap mosel (Klusserather St Michael 1990), an excellent value auslese (Flonheimer Adelberg 1990), and a couple of amusing Americans (Glen Ellen Chardonnay 1991 and the mouth-puckeringly weird red Inglenook Charbono referred to above).

The store's philosophy, and it has one, can be summed up in its self-proclaimed understanding and commitment to the high street. Recognizing that other supermarket groups are developing larger and larger out-of-town sites, mainly serving car owners or those who can be fagged to lug shopping on

public transport, Budgen has concentrated on town centres
and adjacent shopping areas. Doubtless, many older folk and
those who do not or care not to drive, and those who merely
need to nip out to buy something rather than indulge in a full
or near-full weekly shop, find such a store of great benefit.
The wine drinker has not been left out of this scenario and
whilst there is not a huge staff of wine buyers at the store's
HQ, one brave man being all I have ever met, the world of
wine is fairly represented on its shelves and it will, I reckon,
get better and better.

AUSTRALIAN WINE – *red*

Jacob's Creek Dry Red	13	£C
Penfolds Bin 389 Cabernet/Shiraz	13	£D

AUSTRALIAN WINE – *white*

Riverina/Budgen South East Australia Semillon	12	£B

AUSTRIAN WINE – *white*

Winzerhaus Grüner Veltliner 1991   14   £C
At under £4 this is a bargain. Lots of fruit, good acidity, and
overall modernity. Its style astonishes many people.

CHILEAN WINE – *red*

Underraga Pinot Noir 1989   10   £B
Intense strawberry and cherry aroma fronts a wine which
disappoints in the bleakness of its fruit after such a promising
start.

FRENCH WINE – *red*

Abbaye St-Hilaire, Côteaux Varois, Listel 1990   12   £B
Good style wine.

Château Bassanel Minervois 1991   12   £B
Real peasant style.

Château de la Jaubertie   13   £C
A consistently good wine made by ex-stationery magnate Nick
Ryman in the Dordogne. Has admirable structure and depth
of fruit.

Château de Malijay, Côtes du Rhône 1991   11   £C
Odd, very odd. Looks and tastes like Tierra del Fuegoan
pinot noir.

Claret, Dulong (Budgen)   13   £B
Good style wine.

Côtes du Rhône Villages   13   £C

Delas Crozes-Hermitage   10   £C

Faugères, Jean Jean   13   £C
Very meaty. Great pasta wine.

**Le Haut Colombier, Vin de Pays de la
Drôme 1992** 13 £B
Touch of sweet fruit to it. It has a real Rhône-style structure
and feel.

Madiran, Domaine de Fitère 12 £C
Good cheap claret type.

Vin de Pays des Coteaux de l'Ardèche 1991 12 £B
Nice dry cherry fruit.

FRENCH WINE – *white and rosé*

Blanc de Blancs Cuveé Speciale 10 £B

Blanc de Blancs Sur Lie, Listel 1991 12 £B

Chablis Domaine St-Marc 1988 10 £D

Château Fondarzac 13 £B

Château Le Gordonne, Côtes de Provence Rosé 13 £C
Pleasant summer rosé (dry) with strawberry bubble-gum
aftertaste.

Corbières Blanc de Blancs 1990 13 £B
Outright bargain. Not as determinedly keen-edged as it might
be but attractively fruity all the same in a quiet way.

Domaine de Bosquet-Canet, Listel 11 £C

Domaine de Villeroy-Castellas, Listel 1991 13 £C

Gewürztraminer Gisselbrecht 1989 14 £C
Expensive but lovely. Spicy lychee fruit plus clean acidity.

**Le Bonnefois, Vin de Pays de Côtes de
Gascogne**   13   £B
Delicious fruit. Very good value.

Muscadet Sur Lie, Beauregard 1989   11   £B

**Muscadet Sur Lie, Domaine du Bois Breton
1991**   10   £C
Typically woolly muscadet. Some fruit.

Muscat, Vin de Pays Catalan   11   £B

Pinot Blanc Gisselbrecht   12   £C

Sancerre, Les Grand Dames 1990   11   £D

Tuilerie du Bosc, Côtes de Saint-Mont 1991   13   £C
One of the best white wines for the money in the store.
Well-stratified fruit, good balance. Terrific little wine.

GERMAN WINE – *white*

Bereich Bernkastel 1991   11   £B

Erben Kabinett 1991 (1 litre)   11   £C

Flonheimer Adelberg Auslese   14   £C
Delicious aperitif; lemony undertones, touched with honey.
Fantastic value.

Klusserather St Michael Kabinett 1990   13   £B
Real riesling character, tone, lemonic and characterful.

Longuicher Probstberg Kabinett   11   £C

HUNGARIAN WINE – *red*

Cabernet Sauvignon	13	£B
Merlot	12	£B

HUNGARIAN WINE – *white*

Chardonnay	10	£B
Sauvignon Blanc	10	£B

ITALIAN WINE – *red*

Barolo Cortese   13   £C
Rich liquorice, cherries and blackcurrant – and a little spice.
Yet soft. A fancy slurp.

Chianti Classico, Castelgreve 1989   11   £C

ITALIAN WINE – *white*

Lugana Villa Flora 1991   15   £C
An elegant, balanced wine of great coolness of character and
somewhat haughty class. Bags of style for less than bags of
money.

MORAVIAN WINE – *white*

Château Valtice Pinot Blanc   8   £B
This is Czech republic wine and so republicans, and ex-
Marxists, may find it interesting. It is quite absurd the place
dares to affix the word château to itself as it is merely a winery
and I can record that I had a noteworthy lunch there in the
workers' canteen: I was offered nary a glass of any of their
wines during my meal, not even a glass of water. I often
wonder about this. Winery apart, Valtice is an interesting little
ex-Habsburgian hang-out, with its vineyards edging the
Austrian border, and is well worth exploring.

NEW ZEALAND WINE – *red*

Montana Cabernet Sauvignon   12   £C

NEW ZEALAND WINE – *white*

Villa Maria Sauvignon Blanc 1991   14   £C
Like a fruitier sancerre. Really quite distinguished drinking.

PORTUGUESE WINE – *red*

Dão Dom Ferraz 13 £B
Great fast-food wine. But then Mr Ferraz is an incredibly fast
driver.

Tinto de Anfora 1988 14 £D
One of the classiest and most satisfying wines of Portugal, and
in a great vintage not available everywhere (it has been
replaced by the '89). Made from satin and figs by an Australian.

PORTUGUESE WINE – *white*

Vinho Verde 10 £B

SOUTH AFRICAN WINE – *red*

Table Mountain 1991 14 £B
An excellent, thorough-going bargain. Tastes exactly like
Waitrose's Far Enough 1991 (which see, page 247).

SPANISH WINE – *red*

Don Carvi Navarra 13 £B

Marqués de Cáceres   13   £C
One of less hysterical riojas. Refined, rather than full-
blooded.

Raimat Tempranillo   14   £D
Utterly ravishing wine of deep richness and suave fruit.

Viña Albali 1983   14   £B
This great wine bargain pops up on wine shelves all over the
place, and in various vintages. This has oodles of fruit and is
just perfect with all sorts of rich foods.

USA WINE – *white*

Glenn Ellen Proprietor's Reserve Chardonnay   15   £C
Gorgeous style – buttery chardonnay (in the Aussie mould)
with a touch of New Zealand citricity. Delightful Californian
sum of the parts.

Inglenook Charbono   14   £C
Madeira-coloured, dry as charcoal, some dried curranty fruit.
Interesting specimen of a rare breed. Probably good with
spicy sausages as burnt as it is.

SPARKLING WINE/CHAMPAGNE

Lindauer, New Zealand   13   £D
Good fizzer.

Paul Cheneau Cava   8   £D

Co-op

The woman who runs the Co-op's wine buying department also runs marathons. One exhausting long haul followed by another, the cynic might say. However, such a cynic is out of touch and will have to swallow his words: the dear old Co-op has an awful lot going for it these days. The wines are neither dear nor old. The idea, held by even the most unassuming of wine drinkers, that a trip to buy wine at the Co-op is as unlikely a venture as visiting a nuclear power station canteen for lunch, is out of date. Youth, freshness and good value for money is their hallmark. Even their unprepossessingly titled English Table Wine surprises with its attractive fragrance and summons up, both in its aroma and taste, a quintessentially English image of broad swathes of lawn, spring flowers, and strawberry fields. This white wine costs £4.19 and rates 14 points.

The Co-op isn't like other stores which can dictate which wines are stocked by individual branches. Regional Co-ops are free to buy what they wish and often this does not include the wines listed here. This is a great pity and one instance where I am totally in favour of centralized decision-making. If only the Co-op's vast popularity as a retailer was matched by a single-minded approach to its purchasing and marketing methods where wine is concerned, it could become a formidable force in supermarketing. It's doubtless with a great deal of relief that the Tescos, Safeways and Sainsburys of this world, not to mention Asda and Gateway, do not have the sleeping giant that is the Co-op breathing down the necks of their wine departments. But one day . . . who knows?

AUSTRALIAN WINE – *red*

Cabernet Sauvignon   13   £C
Great with a richly stuffed roast fowl.

Shiraz   14   £C
Famous bruising Aussie style.

BULGARIAN WINE – *red*

Cabernet Sauvignon   11   £B

BULGARIAN WINE – *white*

Welschriesling and Misket   12   £B

CHILEAN WINE – *white*

Sauvignon Blanc   13   £B
Good value for a simple fruity wine. Somewhat quiet to finish
but a very likeable style.

ENGLISH WINE – *white*

English Table Wine   14   £C
The sort of wine the civilized Englishwoman has sitting in an
ice-bucket by her deckchair as she prunes the roses. A quintessentially English wine, forsooth, in the way it summons up
images of lawns. Is that the distant thwack of a tennis ball I
hear? (Funny, what you can get out of a glass of wine.)

FRENCH WINE – *red*

Anjou Rouge   12   £C

Bergerac Rouge   13   £B

Cahors   14   £C
Made by the highly regarded Rigal brothers who are *négociants*
as well as making their own wine at Château St-Didier in
Parnac. This wine is blackcurrant and coal tar and is well dry
yet has soft fruit – indeed the smiling softness of the fruit is
curiously counterpointed by a typical scowl of Cahors dryness
and the whole adds up to a pleasantly balanced personality.

Charles Vienot Côtes du Beaune Villages   12   £D

Château Cissac 1982   12   £E

Château Cissac 1984   11   £E

Château Laurençon, Bordeaux Supérieur 1989 14   £C
Delightful soft tannins yet great ageing potential nevertheless.
Those dry blackberries in the wine will just get prettier and
prettier. (Say two–three years?)

**Châteauneuf-du-Pape, Cellier des Princes
1989** 11 £E

Claret 12 £B

Corbières 11 £B

Costières de Nîmes 13 £B
Earthy, soft, dry, edgily nutty with blackcurrant and plum fuit.

Côtes de Provence Rouge 12 £B

Côtes du Luberon 13 £B
Attractive, gentle charcoal/rubber bouquet, plus a good dollop
of cheering fruit. Good value.

Côtes du Rhône 11 £B

Côtes du Roussillon 11 £B

Côtes du Ventoux 11 £B

Domaine de Hautrive, Côtes du Rhône Villages 12 £C

Fitou 12 £B

Mâcon Rouge 12 £C

Médoc 12 £C

Morgon, Les Charmes 1990 12 £D
A good cru wine in many respects.

Vacqueyras, Cuvée du Marquis de Fonseguille 14 £D
Soft, approachable, utterly plum-in-the mouth well-speaking
for a downtrodden Rhône bumpkin. Most attractive dry finish.

Vin de Pays de Cassan 14 £B
Cheap, fruity, supple, soft. Wonderfully drinkable. Stylis-
tically, chianti meets côtes-du-rhône.

| Vin de Pays de l'Aude | 11 | £B |
| Vin de Table Red | 11 | £B |

FRENCH WINE – *white and rosé*

Alsace Gewürztraminer   14   £D
Lychee and grapefruit to the nose, mulled fruit, richly edged
for the mouth, spicy tickle in the throat. An interesting aperitif, or to drink solo with a book, or for mild Chinese food.

Alsace Pinot Blanc	13	£C
Alsace Riesling	10	£C
Anjou Blanc	13	£C
Bergerac Blanc	11	£B
Blanc de Blancs	11	£B
Bordeaux Blanc Medium Dry	12	£B
Bourgogne Blanc	10	£D
Côtes de Provence Rosé	10	£C

Côtes du Roussillon (Vignerons Catalans)   13   £B
No great depth or sophistication but utterly guzzlable.
Attractive melon fruit (totally predictably) but with a good
balancing acidity (not so predictably).

Muscadet Sur Lie, Dormaine Breuillet 1990   13   £C
Decent muscadet is rarer than hen's teeth nowadays so this is
an exception: farmyard vegetal aroma, attractive fruit, fresh
finish. Great with shellfish.

Premières Côtes de Bordeaux	11	£B
Rosé d'Anjou A pleasant little rosé.	12	£B
Vin de Pays d'Oc Sauvignon Blanc	13	£B
Vin de Pays de la Vallée du Paradis Grenache	13	£B
Vin de Pays des Côtes de Gascogne	12	£B
Vin de Pays des Côtes des Pyrénées Orientales	13	£B
Vouvray, Domaine Les Perruches 1990 Good off-dry aperitif.	12	£D

GERMAN WINE – *white*

Bereich Nierstein	12	£B
Bernkasteler Kurfustlay	12	£B
Hock Deutscher Tafelwein	11	£B
Liebfraumilch	10	£B
Mosel Deutscher Tafelwein	11	£B
Moseltaler	11	£B
Niersteiner Gutes Domtal (1.5 litres)	13	£D
Oppenheimer Krotenbrunnen	11	£B
Piesporter Michelsberg	12	£B
Rudesheimer Rosengarten	12	£B

Trocken Rheinpfalz   14 £B
A bargain at just over £3. Attractive fragrance of green grass
and lemon. Good weight of fruit, balanced, fresh to finish.

ITALIAN WINE – *red*

Barbera del Piemonte   14 £B
Strawberry and blackberry crumble, prior to baking. Subtle
acidity, very dry – a quiet, rather than typically exuberant
barbera, but hugely drinkable and no ugly bits showing. Terrific value.

Chianti	10	£B
Merlot del Veneto	13	£B

Cherries! Who'll buy my sweet cherries?!

Valpolicella	12	£A
Valpolicella Classico Superiore 1988	12	£C

Some attractive cherry fruit but very light.

ITALIAN WINE – *white*

Bianco di Custoza   12 £C
Nice-ish weight of fruit, fair-ish balance, fresh-ish finish. If
like your wine with lots of ish, this ish for you.

Frascati	10	£B
Frascati Superiore	11	£C

Orvieto Secco	12	£C

Soave	10	£A

Trebbiano dell'Emilia   13   £B
Excellent value for a calm, unfussy wine useful as an aperitif
or with mild fish dishes.

Verdicchio Classico	12	£C

PORTUGUESE WINE – *red*

Bairrada Tinto 1987   15   £B
Compelling aroma of currants (slightly porty), rich yet never
sweaty fruit, and a forceful finish. Great partner for richer
dishes. And brilliant value.

Douro   15   £B
Another wonderful slurp from the land of happy smiling
peasant wines (pricewise) which have rich aristocratic natures
(tastewise). Lovely blackberry fruit here.

Smith Woodhouse 10-year-old Tawny Port   15   £E
Tawny in name but not in nature: vigorous, lean, beautifully
blushing, unbloody and unbowed by its time in cask which
failed to darken its cheeks or diminish its fruity, nutty, curranty character which will partner cheese brilliantly. Worth
the money to experience one glass.

Vinho de Mesa Santos   15   £B
Typical baked figs and earth aromatically which completely
belie the creamy fruit flavour. Delicious. Astoundingly good
value.

PORTUGUESE WINE – *white and rosé*

Bairrada Branco   15   £B
The white wine drinker's oldest ally in times of scarce coinage
and violent recession. Fantastic value here: nutty yet fresh,
slightly subdued aromatically, but admirably well balanced
with a lush, soft fruit flavour set off by the acidity. Interesting
bitter lemon finish.

Portuguese Rosé   10   £B

Vinho Verde   11   £B

SPANISH WINE – *red*

Rioja   12   £C

SPARKLING WINE/CHAMPAGNE

Cava   11   £C

De Clairveaux Brut Champagne   13   £F
Some style here.

De Clairveaux Rosé Champagne   12   £G

Liebfraumilch   10   £C

Sparkling Saumur   13   £D
An apple/peach/pear sparkler of some style.

Gateway/Somerfield

The Gateway/Somerfield annual wine tasting was held this year at the Café Royal. That's confidence for you. But then even when she is still officially on maternity leave the person who runs the store's wine-buying department has confidence in her taste, and enough energy and commitment to run the department from home, and the wines in this book fully justify this attitude. There's an interesting new range of English wines, some smashing own-label cheap Aussies, a pack of interesting Italians, a most attractive pink sparkling wine at a daft price, and some terrific Spanish, Portuguese and Chilean bottles.

Over the year, the store has had some good £1.99 bottles too, on promotional special offer, and there is no doubt that this store is beginning to bear little resemblance, wine-wise, to the one I first began to write about five years back. Indeed, some months ago, early one Saturday morning, I was telephoned by a distinguished food writer of my acquaintance who found himself in Wales for the weekend. 'Help!' he cried. 'I must take my hostess some decent wines for my weekend here and all I can find locally is a Gateway. Am I in luck or not?' I told him he was. And I told him he wasn't. If the branch stocked the following wines, and I reeled off half-a-dozen cheapo little Gateway marvels I knew of, he *was* in luck. But if the branch was a small one, he would be lucky to find any of them. I know this for a fact because *Guardian* readers do occasionally write and ask me if the Gateway store I have written about which has some particularly wonderful wine I've recommended is the same Gateway store as the one they have locally but which disclaims all knowledge of the wine in

45

question. In other words, you need to find a Gateway with a
damn decent wine department to find the fullest range of the
best wines. My friend was in luck, as it happened. He found
four of the six wines I mentioned, bought them, and was
considered a wildly generous and deliciously discerning guest
for his pains. And that pain, by his own admission to me later,
was well short of twenty quid.

ARGENTINIAN WINE – *red*

Trapiche Cabernet Sauvignon Reserve 1990   14   £C
Delicious, soft, drily finished.

AUSTRALIAN WINE – *red*

Australian Red (Somerfield)   14   £B
A very unlikely but nevertheless very attractive Australian.
Terrific soft fruit and terrific value.

Basedows Shiraz   14   £C
Smashing ripe fruit.

**Berri Estates Barossa Valley Cabernet
Sauvignon 1987**   16   £C
This wine went brilliantly with lettuce and almond salad,
cockle soup, cold sturgeon and veal and ham pie in the cook
book that I was reading while guzzling this wine, and the
extraordinary blackcurrant and liquorice fruit never flagged
once. Highly aromatic, with an intense savoury flavour, rubbery and velvety at the same time, it has supple wood and

grape tannins well-integrated with the acidity – an ambrosial
libation which bruises the tongue and lashes the throat.

Cabernet Sauvignon	15	£C
Leathery, soft, brilliant. Gorgeous fruit.		

Château Reynella Cabernet Sauvignon 1988 13 £D

Hardys Grenache/Shiraz (Somerfield) 12 £B

Koonunga Hill Shiraz/Cabernet 1991 14 £C
Masterly, for under a fiver.

Mount Hurtle Cabernet Sauvignon/Merlot 12 £C
Pricey, delicious, very fresh fruit and very un-Aussie.

Penfolds Bin 389 Cabernet/Shiraz 13 £E
Excellent stuff.

Seaview Cabernet Sauvignon 12 £C

Seaview Cabernet/Shiraz 13 £C

Shiraz 1990 (Somerfield) 14 £C
Excellent. Not as spicy as some, but luscious soft fruit.

Shiraz/Cabernet (Somerfield) 1991 15 £C
Under four quid, this is a brilliant wine – absolutely knock-
out stuff.

AUSTRALIAN WINE – *white*

Australian Dry White (Somerfield) 15 £B
Delicious, not shrieking with fruit but definitely announcing it
clearly and cleanly. Fantastic value.

Basedows Semillon 13 £C

Fermented in a marsupial's pouch, this wine cannot help but be leathery, oily, motherly. It smothers you with so many wet kisses one glass is overwhelmingly sufficient.

Chardonnay (Somerfield) 13 £C

Koonunga Hill Chardonnay 14 £C

Excellent. Delightful rich fruit well kitted out with flashes of acidity and one of the most consistently endearing Aussie chardies on sale under a fiver.

Penfolds Padthaway Chardonnay 1990 14 £E

Captivating cocktail: oil, fruit and citric sauce. Smashing stuff.

AUSTRIAN WINE – *white*

Winzerhaus Grüner Veltliner 1991 14 £C

CHILEAN WINE – *red*

Santa Rita Reserve Cabernet Sauvignon 14 £C

Delightful plum fruit, quite soft yet dry, well balanced. An attractive wine.

CHILEAN WINE – *white*

Peteroa Sauvignon Blanc 13 £B

ENGLISH WINE – *white*

Denbies Surrey Gold 1990   13 £D
Honeyed finish of artificial rotundity spoils what could be one
of the finest English wines made. Has many admirable qualities
but it is an unnecessarily fat wine (and a rather expensive one).
It's built to do well in professional tasting rooms but in the most
important room of all, the dining, it lacks the acidity to compel
the drinker to a second glass. Shame.

Elmham Park 1991   13 £D
A lively union between madeleine angevin and kerner grape
varieties and classified medium dry – whatever that means. I
find it a most acceptable aperitif.

Halfpenny Green Seyval Blanc   13 £C
Has an attractive lemon sherbet fruitiness and is an excellent
addition to the album of any member of the Royal Society for
the Collection of Really Awful Labels.

Lamberhurst Sovereign   13 £B
Appley and sweet melon fruit. Some freshness. Good aperitif
and garden party wine.

Pilton Dry   13 £C
If this is dry then I'm a monkey's uncle.

Regatta, Valley Vineyards 1991   14 £C
Delicious, fresh, and well balanced with glints of gooseberry
streaking through the fruit.

Three Choirs English House   14 £B
Greater richness of fruit than most English wines and much
better balanced acidically. Certainly an opening bat for the
English Vineyard Association eleven.

FRENCH WINE – *red*

Beaujolais (Somerfield)	10	£C
Beaujolais-Villages, Duboeuf	12	£C
Beaune 1988	12	£E
Bergerac (Somerfield)	13	£B
Brouilly, Duboeuf	12	£C

Cairranne, Domaine des Coteaux de Travers 1991 — 13 £C

Château Barbe-Blanche 1987 — 14 £D
A supple, rather drier than normal St-Em, offering easy drinking and fruity approachability at a reasonable price.

Château Citran 1987 — 13 £E
Bordeaux's worst label but very far from being the region's worst wine. Dry, woody, toasty fruit with a luxuriant elegance.

Château de Caraguilhes, Corbières — 14 £B

Château de la Liquière, Faugères 1991 — 13 £C
Very individual wine: chewy with dry-edged fruit, it will come alive with roast meat and vegetables.

Château la Chapelle Baradis, Côtes de Castillon 1990 — 10 £C

Château La Rocheraie, Bordeaux Supérieur 1989 — 10 £C

Château La Terrasse, Côtes de Castillon — 13 £C
A mature bordeaux, typically tannic, but showing no graceless hardness. Very good value.

Château Saint-Robert, Graves 1987   13   £C
Nice style, nice price. Dry and fruity with a distant hint of the
cedarwood aroma of fine Graves.

Château Talence 1987   13   £C

Châteauneuf-du-Pape, La Solitude   13   £E

Chinon, Pierre Chainier   12   £D

Claret (Somerfield)   12   £B

Côtes de Gascogne   12   £A

Côtes de Roussillon Villages   12   £B

Côtes de Duras   13   £B
You can pick up some attractive fruit here for not a lot of
money.

Côtes du Marmandais   12   £B

Côtes du Ventoux (Somerfield)   12   £B

Domaine de Bonserine, Côte-Rotie 1989   10   £G

Domaine de la Solitude, Côtes du Rhône 1991   11   £C

Domaine de St-Julien   13   £B
Good price for Vin de Pays de l'Hérault with decent cabernet
sauvignon character.

Haut-Poitou Gamay 1992   11   £C

Hautes Côtes de Beaune 1991   11   £C

La Pelissière, Cahors 1992   12   £B

Marsannay   13   £D

Médoc   11   £B

Merlot, Domaine de la Magdelaine	13	£C
Minervois, Jean Jean	12	£A
Philippe de Baudin Merlot, Vin de Pays d'Oc 1982	11	£C
Red Burgundy 1990	12	£D
St-Chinian	13	£B

St-Joseph 1989   15   £D
One of the siren-like beauties of the Rhône designed to lure drinkers to their doom (i.e. you become a slave to the wine). Lots of dark rich fruit with an edge like a cheroot. The fumacious tippler will adore it. So will cuckolds – Joseph being, of course, their patron saint.

Santenay 1990   12   £E

Vacqueyras Vieux Clocher 1990   14   £C
Dry earth, damsons and black cherries. A smashing little Rhône beauty.

FRENCH WINE – *white and rosé*

Bordeaux Sauvignon (Somerfield)	12	£B
Chablis 1990 (Somerfield)	13	£D

Chardonnay, Vin de Pays de l'Ardèche   13   £C
Speaks French with an Australian accent.

Chardonnay, Vin de Pays de l'Hérault   13   £C

Château Bastor-Lamontagne 1989 (half)   14   £D
A useful half-bottle at a less than useful price, but this is a
gorgeous pudding wine.

Château du Chayne, Bergerac   12   £C

Château Tour de Montredon, Corbières   14   £B
Nicely put together and terrific value.

Domaine de la Bouletière Rosé 1992   14   £B
This is an organic rosé from the well-known and well-praised
– at least by me – Château Caraguilhes in Corbières. Delightfully perfumed, it has a cheery and very cheering side to it.

Domaine de Marignan, Côtes de Thau   13   £B

Domaine des Garbes, Premières Côtes de
Bordeaux   13   £C

Domaines Grassa 1992 (Somerfield)   13   £B
Luscious touches of fruit to this attractive vin de pays des
Côtes de Gascogne.

Hautes Côtes de Beaune 1991   12   £D

Meursault, Jaffelin 1990   13   £G
The real thing: musty, green and rich – concentrated ripe
melonness.

Montagny Premier Cru 1989   12   £D

Sancerre, Les Chanvières   12   £D

Vin de Pays des Coteaux de L'Ardèche Blanc   13   £B
Terrific value. Very clean. Good with shellfish.

White Burgundy (Somerfield)   12   £C

GERMAN WINES – *white*

Dornfelder Trocken St Ursula	13	£C
Baden Dry	13	£B

**Bodenheimer Burgweg Juwel Beerenauslese
1989 (half)**   14 £D
With a slice of fruit tart or an apple and a hunk of cheese this
wine is a jewel indeed. Alas, it's over a fiver for the half bottle
which is an angelic size for such a wine but a devilish price
tag, though it is beautifully stratified sipping, with layers of
herby honey-tinged fruit wound around subtle orange and
lime peel flavouring.

Niersteiner Spiegelberg 1991	12	£B
Oberemmeler Rosenberg Riesling 1989	11	£D
St Johanner Abtei Kabinett	12	£B
St Ursula Weinkellerei Bingen Morio Muskat	11	£A
St Ursula Weinkellerei Bingen Pinot Blanc Trocken Gallerei Range	11	£B
St Ursula Weinkellerei Bingen Rheingau Riesling	11	£B
Trocken (Somerfield)	13	£B

HUNGARIAN WINE – *red*

Bull's Blood	13	£B

HUNGARIAN WINE – *white*

Gyöngyös Estate Dry Muscat 1992 Pleasant aperitif.	13	£B

ITALIAN WINE – *red*

Barolo, Castiglione Faletto	12	£D
Cabernet Sauvignon del Veneto	11	£B
Carignan del Sulcis A lot of very attractive fruit here.	13	£C
Chianti, Conti Serristori	13	£B
Copertino 1990 Excellent value for money for utterly simple, dry, fruity wine drinking which is incomparably unpretentious and satisfying.	14	£B
Librandi Ciro 1990	12	£C
Montereale	13	£B
Riserva di Fizzano, Chianti Classico	13	£E
Rosso de Braganze 1991	13	£C
Salice Salentino 1986 Rich, mature, figgy fruit.	13	£C
Vignetti Casterna Valpolicella Classico 1990	13	£C
Vino Nobile di Montelpulciano 1989 A most compellingly fruity wine.	14	£D

ITALIAN WINE – *white*

Caldeo 1990   13   £B
Lemons and raspberries – a subtle fruit salad set off by a dash
of Venetian acidity. Delicious value for money.

Frascati, Principe Pallavicini (Somerfield)   12   £C

Montereale 1991   13   £B

Pinot Bianco del Veneto   12   £B

Pinot Grigio del Veneto   12   £B

Terre di Ginestra   13   £C
One of the classiest white wines to come out of Sicily in recent
years, though I can't say I'm overjoyed at its proximity to a
fiver. A lean wine very good with crustacea and grilled fish.

LEBANESE WINE – *red*

Château Musar 1985   15   £E
This wine is in the luxury class as a mouthful of volatile, spicy,
velvety fruit, quite superb with a richly stuffed bird but, alas, it
is now touching the luxury class in price.

PORTUGUESE WINE – *red*

Caves Velhas Garrafeira 1990   13   £D

Dão Reserva 1987   14 £B
Ooh . . . lashings of lovely baked fruit at a give-away price.

Lezíria   14 £B
One of the brightest wine bargains on earth. Perfect for pastas
and pizzas or even stone soup (which is one of the specialities
of the region where the wine is made) and this remarkably
fruity and delicious wine can, let me tell you, cope brilliantly
with stones of all sizes, shapes and flavours. Indeed, it is a gem
of a wine for the money.

Planicie   15 £B
Rippling tippling. Delicious cherries and plums, dry yet
rounded. A shimmeringly attractive wine for a silly amount of
money – from one of the Portugal's brightest co-ops, opposite
the bullring in Almeirim.

Quinta da Pancas 1990   13 £D
This is an attractive wine, made by an immensely attractive
man who lives in a fabulously attractive house with wooden
ceilings. His family have been making wine at their *quinta* for
500 years, so he merits our respect – but I do wish this red of
his was at least £1.50 cheaper than it is.

PORTUGUESE WINE – *white and rosé*

Bairrada Rosé 1992   13 £B
A pleasant summery rosé with an aroma of particular appeal,
appropriately, to rose growers. Excellent price.

Bairrada, Caves Aliança   13 £B

SOUTH AFRICAN WINE – *red*

Cape Selection Pinotage 1991   13   £B
Good value for stacks of gooey fruit.

SOUTH AFRICAN WINE – *white*

Chenin Blanc, Simonsvlei   13   £B
This is strictly for rice and fish dishes.

SPANISH WINE – *red*

Don Hugo   14   £B
Great bargain boozing for spicy sausages and curries.

Ochoa Tempranillo 1988   14   £D
Lovely deep fruit, richly shaped. Delicious with offal like liver
and bacon or cheese on toast with bits of sun-dried tomatoes
embedded.

Palacio de León 1986   15   £C
A very deserving bottle – a good rich stew should do it. This
león has great fruit (dry yet vibrant), is well balanced, and has
a finish of nutty figs with a touch of chocolate.

Rioja Alemenar 1990   15   £C
The price isn't a lot nowadays for wine of this downright
delicious sort which isn't so hefty and hyped-up with wood
that it begs for food; this rioja is most enjoyable by itself,

having lightly oaked, savoury fruit of a very soft variety (but be
damned if I can tell you which), and I would guess that there's
a good deal of the garnacha grape variety (Spanish grenache)
along with the tempranillo and this makes for a very smooth
landing on the tongue.

Señorio de Agos, Rioja Reserva 1987   11   £D

Señorio de Val 1988   15   £B
What a ridiculous price! Beautiful vanilla, coconut, banana
woodiness and lengthy blackcurrant fruit. For all that, a dry
wine and quite delicious.

Viña Albali Gran Reserva 1984   14   £B
It's creamy, vanillary, blackcurranty, and rather forceful.
Drink with dishes equally characterful.

Viña Ardanza Rioja Reserva 1985   12   £E

SPANISH WINE – *white*

Don Hugo Blanco   14   £B
Vanilla and coconut fruit and grapefruity acidity. Great with a
fish curry.

Rioja Blanco   12   £C

Rioja Blanco Mariscol 1988   13   £C

Valencia Dry White   13   £B

USA WINE – *red*

Californian Red (Somerfield)   13   £B
Very good value.

Glen Ellen Cabernet Sauvignon 1988   13   £C

Glen Ellen Merlot 1991   13   £C
Not yet in the class of '90 which rated 16.

Sebastiani Zinfandel   14   £C
Delicious savory mélange of dry berries.

USA WINE – *white*

Sebastiani Chardonnay   13   £C

YUGOSLAVIAN WINE – *red*

Pinot Noir 1989   10   £B
Still listed by the store as a Yugoslavian wine in spite of the fact that this appellation no longer applies.

SPARKLING WINE/CHAMPAGNE

Cava, Conde de Caralt (Somerfield)   15   £C
One of the best value sparklers for under a fiver in Britain.

Terrific wine and knocks many a witless champagne speechless.

Chardonnay Santi Vino Spumante Brut   13   £C
Excellent aperitif sparkler.

Crémant de Bourgogne, Cave de Lugny   13   £D
Excellent structure. Good balance. Very good value.

Lindauer Brut   13   £E
What a pity it's a touch over £7! Still, it's a delicious lemon sparkler for all that.

Moscato Fizz   13   £A

Prince William Blanc de Blancs   13   £G

Prince William Brut Reserve Champagne   13   £F

Prince William Brut Rosé Champagne   13   £G
Not a bad rosé, as rosés go.

Touraine Rosé   16   £D
A richly aromatic wine, with a mature, elegantly fruity feel balanced by an assertive acidity (as a good sparkler must be to be refreshing and second-glass-inviting), and it is a serious champagne sub: classy, distinguished and extremely good value for money.

Vouvray, Tête de Cuvée   14   £D
Knock-out champagne sub.

Kwik Save

This is a newcomer to the *Superplonk* book and, on the face of it, an unlikely store for wine lovers. But the fact is that Kwik Save have in recent months got themselves an experienced wine consultant, Angela Muir, and through her good offices, taste and skill, got a few good wines on shelf. Price is the key at Kwik Save (with a name like that you could hardly expect anything else) and they claim to have lower prices than anyone – but then a lot of supermarkets do that. However, it's true that the admirable Lezíria is actually less than £1.99 here (or was at the time this book went to press) and tuppence saved is tuppence earned and so at £1.97 this must be the cheapest drinkable wine in the land. Curiously, though, not everyone thinks this sort of thing is admirable in the least: I was much amused at the tasting Ms Muir arranged for wine writers to overhear one stalwart of the wine-spitting fraternity wondering aloud to herself just who on earth drank some of the wines on show and what did such drinkers expect for such low prices? The answer is drinkable wines and, in some cases, very drinkable wines indeed.

The impetus to Kwik Save developing a wider interest in wine, other than the usual branded bottles found everywhere, was the store's purchase two years ago of the Liquorsave franchise business. As grocers, they had a healthy 10 per cent of the market but only a fraction of this was wine. With 780 stores throughout England and Wales and a proclaimed commitment to expand, with the involvement of a consultant with particular skills at buying and developing inexpensive wines, they are a retailer to watch. Certainly I shall watch them and I expect the restricted entry below to expand as the group does.

Kwik Save obviously has its *raison d'être* and this is to sell branded household goods cheaper than other people with no frills and hardly any thrills except the age-old one of saving money. But if Ms Muir can increase the number of very attractive, fruity, and very cheap wines like Comtesse de Lorancy (see entry) then Kwik Save can become a very interesting place indeed.

AUSTRALIAN WINE – *white*

Angove's Chardonnay 1992	13	£C
Coldridge Estate Semillon/Chardonnay 1992	13	£B

FRENCH WINE – *red*

Beaujolais 1992   13   £B
Some delicate fruit at a reasonable price.

Cabernet Sauvignon, Vin de Pays d'Oc   13   £A
Dry, serious, good value.

Château Jougrand, St-Chinian 1991   13   £C

Côtes du Rhône 1992   13   £B
Good value here.

Domaine Resclause Merlot 1992   14   £B
Particularly rich and fruity and superb value.

Minervois 1991   11   £A

Rouge de France   12   £A

FRENCH WINE – *white*

Blanc de Blancs Gascogne   14   £B
Delicious pineappley fruit.

Bordeaux Blanc 1992   12   £B

Comtesse de Lorancy   15   £B
Here we not only have the thrill of a wonderfully dated and
utterly repulsive label but an even more deliciously hideous
consideration. Lorancy is what is termed EEC wine. It is a
blend of wines from more than one EEC country, based on
the Spanish airén which is tankered up from La Lancha to
northern France to be blended with a little local sauvignon
and chardonnay. The wine is astonishingly fruity in the melon
mould, well formed, balanced properly with lashings of
friendly acidity, and it is a remarkable bargain for two quid
odd.

Domaine de la Gravenne 1992   13   £B
A vin de pays d'Oc with some very attractive fruit.

Muscadet 1992   10   £B

Sauvignon Blanc 1992   12   £B

HUNGARIAN WINE – *white*

Chardonnay   12   £B

ITALIAN WINE – *red*

Il Paesano, Merlot del Veneto	12	£A
Valpolicella	13	£A

ITALIAN WINE – *white*

Soave	11	£B
Trebbiano delle Marche 1992	11	£B

NEW ZEALAND WINE – *white*

Delegats Hawkes Bay Sauvignon Blanc   14   £C
To sip during the winter to remind you of the fresh cut grass of summer.

Nobilo Poverty Bay Chardonnay 1991   12   £C

PORTUGUESE WINE – *white*

Lezíria   15   £A
One of the greatest under-two-quid white wine bargains on sale. And at this store it's a whole tuppence cheaper than elsewhere!

SOUTH AFRICAN WINE – *red*

Clearsprings Cape   13   £B

SOUTH AFRICAN WINE – *white*

Clearsprings Cape   11   £B

SPANISH WINE – *white*

Castillo de Liria Moscatel   16   £B
Bituminously rich and flavoursome pudding wine. Remarkable value for the Christmas pudding.

USA WINE – *white*

Californian Premium White   13   £B
Some decent fruit here.

SPARKLING WINE/CHAMPAGNE

Great Western Brut, Australia   15   £C
Under a fiver for this? Then hang the champagne!

Littlewoods

I wasn't surprised to meet this store's booze buyer on a trip to Romania I undertook earlier this year. Romania is one hell of a place for bargains at the moment and so it's an excellent hunting ground for retail buyers – especially if you're a store whose customers are uncomfortable spending more than three quid on a bottle of wine. Roughly 48 per cent of this store's range of full-strength still table wines is under three quid and 47 percent is under four. The spendthrift at Littlewoods will find no wine to suit unless he or she goes completely bonkers and spends £17.99 on a bottle of Moët et Chandon champagne – and even that is a couple of quid cheaper than it is at other places.

The range is a quarter of the size of Safeway's and Sainsbury's (and Waitrose's). This is what is known as focused marketing in the trade. Commonsense would say it's merely knowing your customers.

Eastern Europe figures well, with the Romanian Pinot Noir the star, and so does Australia. The own-label champagne, under £11 at time of going to press, is no bad bottle either.

Any surprises? Nope. Well, maybe one ... the Château d'Aigueville Côtes du Rhône Blanc at perilously close to £4 the bottle. Won't set the world alight, but I wouldn't turn down the chance of a glass if you're offering.

There's the expected range of montillas, of course. I suspect montilla does rather well out of Littlewoods. Montilla Cream – sweet, oxidized, and as rich as a well-hung jock strap – is only £2.85 compared, say, with Spanish Cream Sherry at £4.39. What's the difference, the £1.54 apart? Montilla attracts less liquor duty, but is still high in alcohol, and it isn't from Jerez – but it tastes like it comes from there. When it's rich and sweet it's as comforting to the honey-dentured drinker as any sherry, but when it's bone dry, chilled to perishing, and cutting your tongue like a razor it has an acquired taste which is best acquired in its home town of Córdoba. But you might get the hang of montilla's particular appeal with a dish of whelks or cockles. Try it. Littlewoods has a dry one for the same price as the cream.

AUSTRALIAN WINE – *red*

Jacob's Creek Dry Red   13   £C
Full-bodied, but not too overdeveloped – complementary to carnivores' favourites like steak and onions.

Windsor Ridge Cabernet Sauvignon   12   £C
Like a very minor bordeaux in many respects.

Windsor Ridge Shiraz   13   £B
Pleasant touches of mint on the fruit.

AUSTRALIAN WINE – *white*

Jacob's Creek Medium Dry White   11   £B

Windsor Ridge Chardonnay   13   £C
Some good fruit here.

Windsor Ridge Sauvignon Blanc   14   £C
Perfect little sauvignon blanc for the money: fresh, fruity, and eminently respectable.

Windsor Ridge Semillon   13   £B
How long can this pleasant number stay the bargain it is for
under £3?

BULGARIAN WINE – *red*

Bulgarian Cabernet Sauvignon   12   £B

FRENCH WINE – *red*

Château d'Aigueville 1990   13   £C
This is an attractive, if not wholly exciting, wine and it has a
very attractive price tag. It's lighter than many of its neigh-
bours, and takes well to chilling.

Vin de Table Red (Littlewoods)   12   £A

FRENCH WINE – *white and rosé*

Rosé d'Anjou (Littlewoods)   13   £A

Vin de Table Dry (Littlewoods)   10   £A

Vin de Table Medium (Littlewoods)   10   £A

GERMAN WINE – *white*

Hock	11	£A

Morio Muskat	13	£A

A simple aperitif of remarkable acidic/fruit balance. Outstanding value for money.

Mosel Kabinett (1 litre)	11	£C

St Johanner Abtei Auslese	12	£C

HUNGARIAN WINE – *red*

Cabernet Sauvignon	12	£B

Merlot	14	£B

The Villany region's merlot seems to be one of the best bargains of any wine list on which it appears. A great softhearted pasta wine.

HUNGARIAN WINE – *white*

Chardonnay	10	£B

Gewürztraminer	10	£B

This was the wine Attila, sweeping across Hungary's Great Plain, inflicted as the supreme punishment upon those of his warriors who had displeased him. It has improved some since the infamous Hun's time, but only relatively.

Olasz Riesling	12	£B
Sauvignon Blanc	12	£B

ITALIAN WINE – *red*

Chianti Il Borgo	10	£B
Valpolicella	10	£B

ITALIAN WINE – *white*

Frascati	12	£B

A good aperitif wine.

Soave	12	£B

PORTUGUESE WINE – *red*

Bairrada	13	£B

Decently fruity drinking to go with rich poultry dishes.

Dão	13	£B

ROMANIAN WINE – *red*

Romanian Cellars Fetesca Neagra/Cabernet   15   £B
This union between the local grape and the international
variety is a very happy one. The feteasca has a soft earthiness,
sloe-like to taste, whilst the cabernet has bite and backbone
and a blackcurrant quality and the sum of these two parts is
one whole of a wine – a terrific bargain for even posh dinner
tables.

Romanian Pinot Noir   15   £B
The only folk who grumble at this much pungent fruit for
under three quid are pinot noirs growers in other parts of the
world than Romania.

ROMANIAN WINE – *white*

Romanian Cellars Riesling Italico/Muscat   8   £B

SPANISH WINE – *red*

Rioja   13   £C

SPARKLING WINE/CHAMPAGNE

Asti Martini   10   £D
Terribly sweet young thing.

Flutelle   14   £C
Getting close as a whisker to a fiver, this wine. But it's a
pleasant lemony aperitif fizz for all that, and no bad thing to
find in your glass.

Kupferberg Gold   10   £D

Monsigny Champagne (Littlewoods)   15   £F
New blend to this own-label. And it's excellent.

Marks & Spencer

You feel *comfortable* at Marks & Sparks. Does any other store group have a pun made out of its name like that? Shopping at M&S is therapy. Shopping at M&S is safe. It's like sucking your thumb or going to church. With the reputation it has, with the aura that it radiates, and with so many commercial innovations to its credit, I'm surprised it doesn't set up a special phone-line like the Samaritans or 999 which depressed shoppers can ring up and receive solace and aid (and spend only 45p a minute peak time).

For half a century, Marks & Spencer was the most profitable British business of its kind until Sainsbury nicked the title over the '91 and '92 period, but earlier this year it was back on top with profits over £736 million. Undoubtedly, it was able to trade so well during a recession because it was able to buy so well. It wasn't so reliant on overseas supplies as other stores and so the dip in the value of the pound against other currencies meant they could better protect their profit margins. Another reason why they make so much dosh is that they don't discount to the extent that their competitors do and so you'll never see a £1.99 wine at M&S. Value for money, maybe, but cheap wine? Never.

With its 300-odd stores in Britain and Ireland, its weekly average of 15 million customers, and its diversity, it can actually afford to be a touch arrogant – and almost ignore the fact that it has any competition at all. Yet still there is many a wine drinker who would regard the thought of buying his or her wine at M&S as a most odd undertaking indeed. You might buy your fish there (it is, ridiculously, Britain's biggest fishmonger); you would certainly buy the kids their clothes

MARKS & SPENCER   78

there (they sell more than anyone); and bra and knicker buyers rightly regard the place as a shrine (and as a result something like one in three lingerie purchases in Britain are made at M&S). Does that sound the sort of place the wine drinker will find a wide range of interesting bottles? No, it doesn't. Yet even if you're not into knickers or salmon fillets, M&S is still an interesting place to buy wine, even if it isn't the cheapest. The other supermarkets need to have £1.99 bargains on their wine shelves to entice people in and these customers, once their bargain bottle's in the trolley, stop to buy other things, too, and often end up doing their whole weekly shop as a result. M&S, however, builds in a larger profit margin on its wines than do other supermarkets and so even with their legendary trading prowess would find it impossible, I guess, to find an appropriate profit margin on a £1.99 wine. Nevertheless, you can fill two cases with different M&S wine under three quid the bottle, and the drinker for whom this figure is a magic price point will not be disappointed. There's a decent under-£10 champagne on offer but not a sparkling wine of any great shakes under £5 – a definite gap in the range here, I think.

I was pleased to see the store elbowing its Connoisseur's Choice range of wines. This was an upmarket range, with some fancy prices, which attempted to set itself apart and did. But it is not the most winning of marketing ideas, especially in a recession when conspicuous consumption is unfashionable. Pioneering work was done by the store with its two-glass range – an excellent idea for the solo drinker, particularly in a store with so many ready-meals on offer.

However, for sheer innovation, the store's food ideas far outstrip its wine ideas (with the exception of Jeunes Vignes – a delicious declassified chablis for under a fiver). This was not so evident a few years back but now with Safeway and

Sainsbury offering all sorts of interesting blends, grape varieties and buyers' initiatives, and with these stores' wine-buying departments seemingly much freer to strike sudden bargains or make swifter decisions about new and unusual wines (like Safeway's eastern European beauties and Sainsbury's Portuguese and Spanish wines) for under £3 and £4, M&S is not seen to be so hot. Or so competitive.

To be sure, the store still has its under £3 Cuvée du Chapelain and Montepulciano d'Abruzzo, and its £2.99 Chenin Blanc from South Africa and £2.99 Pinot Blanc from Hungary, but the greater excitement, and most of the innovation, is to be found around the £4–5 mark and near–£6 level.

Pity, that.

AUSTRALIAN WINE – *red*

Bin 39 1989 Cabernet Sauvignon   15   £C
An immensely soft-hearted beast which it is only fair to warn readers may well all be sold out by the time this book gets published. It's a wine which has some complexity to its fruit with that typical savoury edge which makes cabernets from this part of the world so attractive and immediately drinkable. Bin 39 is aromatic, offers plums and blackcurrants to taste, has a good length of finish and only pussyfoots around with the acidity. Can't say I'm wild about its proximity to a fiver, but I suppose M&S has a living to make just like the rest of us.

Cabernet Sauvignon Bin 37 Orlando   15   £C
Rich, good balance, lovely berried fruit (mostly black) – overall, a lot of class.

| Cocoparra Reserve Shiraz 1992 | 12 | £B |

| Pheasant Gully Shiraz | 12 | £C |

Shiraz/Cabernet, Mitcheltons 15 £C
Not so menthol-enriched as some examples, this wine is great
stuff with a soft touch of oak to the fruit and a firm style with
the acidity. Very good value.

AUSTRALIAN WINE – *white*

Bin 65 Chardonnay 1991 15 £C
Lovely rich wine with vivid fruit, beautifully defined by the
acidity. Very well made and well priced.

Black Forest Moselle Medium Dry 1992 14 £B
A most unusual and interesting wine. Vegetal aromas, fruit
hitting the roof of the mouth, acidity the floor and the result is
a curiosity of great relevance to salad eaters.

| Cocoparra Reserve Sauvignon Blanc 1992 | 11 | £C |

Hunter Valley Chardonnay/Semillon 1992 13 £C
Quiet, demure, a touch refined – being on M&S shelves has a
funny effect on Aussies.

Len Evans Chardonnay 1991 15 £D
Exuberant with fruit, but not riotous or out of hand – even a
touch delicate, though it's hardly a delicate wine since there is
a rousing, bruising side to the deliciously rich fruit.

| Pheasant Gully Colombard | 12 | £C |

| Semillon/Chardonnay | 13 | £C |

BULGARIAN WINE – *red*

Cabernet Sauvignon Svischtov 1989   13   £B

CHILEAN WINE – *red*

Cabernet Sauvignon 1990   14   £C
No so rampantly minty as previous vintages, this is nevertheless an attractive blackcurranty wine at an excellent price.

CHILEAN WINE – *white*

Chilean Sauvignon Blanc 1991   11   £B

FRENCH WINE – *red*

Beaujolais 1991   12   £C

Beaujolais-Villages, Duboeuf 1991   13   £C

Bouches du Rhône   11   £B

Brouilly 1990   12   £D

Cabernet Sauvignon, Chais Beaucairois   11   £B

Château Le Mounan, Bordeaux 1990   14   £C
Lovely, straightforward structure – woody and teeth-

clingingly dry. Good firm blackcurrants at a surprising price.

Châteauneuf-du-Pape 1991 14 £E
Big-hearted, soft and rich-centred. A confection of great typicality and concentration of flavour. Delicious with rich poultry dishes.

Claret AC (1 litre) 13 £B
Continues to be fair value.

Comte Tolosan 1991 13 £B
Good solid rustic plonking available here at a bargain price.

Côtes de Saint-Mont 1989 13 £B

Côtes du Rhône (1 litre) 13 £C

Domaine de l'Orangerie 1990 13 £B
Very dry, with good brambly fruit, and very good value.

**Domaine St Pierre, Vin de Pays de l'Hérault
1992** 11 £B
Old World/New World dance uneasily hand in hand. Behind the French earthy dryness lurks 'wotcha cobber' pear-and-cherry-drop fruitiness.

Fitou 1989 11 £B

Fleurie 1991 12 £D

French Country 13 £B

Gamay 12 £B

La Petite Propriété, Vin de Pays de l'Aude 1992 12 £B

Margaux, Château Notton 1988 13 £E
This gets more and more drinkable the longer it hangs about

on the shelves but it really ought to be put away on its side for
several years in a cool dark place.

Médoc, Château de Medalli 1989   13   £D

Merlot, Christian Moueix 1989   14   £C
A merlot of some distinction and, for the money, not bad
value since it aspires to be a pedigree bordeaux in feel.

Merlot, Vin de Pays de l'Aude 1992   13   £B
Attractive wine, meaty and rich, but it strains just a little to let
the fruit through. Rather easily bruised when it meets food
but simpleton TV programmes, like a quiz, say, can be swallowed with it.

Rasteau, Côtes du Rhône Villages 1990   14   £C
Somewhat of a hard, woody finish at time of tasting but this
will soften in bottle over the months and the earthiness will
develop into something rather tasty.

Sélection Rouge, Duboeuf 1991   13   £B
Excellent value for money at under three quid. Sound in all
departments.

FRENCH WINE – *white and rosé*

Bouches du Rhône   11   £A

Burgundy, Caves de Lugny 1990   13   £C

Chablis 1990   17   £D
This '90 is superb with enough months under its belt to give it
a mature, almost woody feel, tempered by classic flinty acidity
of subtle smokiness. Ravishingly good and a fantastic bargain
for the price.

Chablis 1991 15 £D
The difference a year makes. An excellent chablis which may well match the '90 given the time.

Chablis, Beauroy Premier Cru 1989 14 £F
Delicious and classic.

Chablis Grand Cru, Château Grenouille 1988 10 £G

Chardonnay, Cellier des Samsons 13 £C

Chardonnay de Chardonnay 13 £C
The eponymous village is the origin of this wine so it's the most authentic chardonnay you can drink, I suppose.

Chasan, Vin de Pays de l'Ardailhou 1992 13 £C
Modern and assertive in style. Good fruit.

Château de Poce, Touraine 13 £C
Some class to the structure.

Côtes de Gascogne 1990 13 £B
Very good value – dry, freshly fruity (not tinned), and harmoniously acidic.

Cuvée du Chapelain 13 £B

French Country 13 £B
Fresh with firm fruit this is excellent value and great with shellfish dishes.

French Medium White (1 litre) 12 £B

Jeunes Vignes 14 £C
This continues to be a decent bottle, in spite of creeping (inevitably) towards a fiver, and with grilled fish or shellfish it is perfect. It is made from declassified chablis vines, officially, but it has been known for the co-op which makes it to bung in

grand cru wine just to keep supplies coming through and
M&S stocked up.

La Charmette Sancerre 1992	10	£D

Les Trois Collines 1991	13	£B

With its melon fruit and dose of friendly acidity, this is a
bargain.

Mâcon Villages 1991	12	£D

**Oliver Mandeville Chardonnay, Vin de Pays
d'Oc 1992**   14   £C
Lush, mellow, buttery fruit: delicious, in a word. Rather New
Worldish in its charms.

Petit Chablis 1992	13	£C

Pinot Blanc d'Alsace	13	£C

Pinot Gris 1990	12	£C

Pouilly-Fumé 1990	12	£D

Rosé d'Anjou (1 litre)	12	£C

Rosé de Syrah 1992   10   £B
Tastes like someone jumped up and down on a packet of
cherry drops – and then vinified the gunge.

Sauvignon de Touraine 1991	13	£C

Sélection Blanc Duboeuf   14   £B
Excellent value for grilled fish dishes. Stylish, balanced, and
most attractive fruit.

GERMAN WINE – *white*

Bereich Nierstein 1991	11	£B
Hock (1 litre)	11	£C
Liebfraumilch	10	£B
Moselle (1 litre)	11	£C
Piesporter Michelsberg 1991	12	£B

HUNGARIAN WINE – *white*

Pinot Blanc 15 £B

In the course of a year I must read and ignore several thousand press releases from PR departments about bottles of wine all of which, naturally enough, say how wonderful the wines are. But one day I received, along with this pinot blanc, a piece of bumf from M&S's PR people which used, I suspect, the store's chief wine buyer's description of the wine. Among other things it said of this pinot that it is 'a fabulous, deliciously juicy, crisp dry white packed with scents of whitecurrants and pears with a zesty, zingy attack on the nostrils. It has ... masses of smooth ripe greengage fruit with a delicate brush of lime acidity in the background for a refreshing mouthwatering balance ... a lovely wine with a silky roundness.' I chuckled and drank and found myself agreeing with everything that was written. Although I can't say my nostrils felt bruised and I did wonder what on earth whitecurrants smelt like.

ISRAELI WINE – *white*

Carmel Valley Colombard 1992	12	£B
Carmel Vineyards Dry Muscat 1992	11	£B

ITALIAN WINE – *red*

Barbera d'Asti 1990   14   £B
A roast beef Italian rather than a spag bol merchant.

Barolo 1987   13   £D
A demure, well-mannered, smooth barolo with little evidence
of the liquorice, figs, and all those rich acrid things this sort of
wine normally abounds in.

Chianti Classico, Villa Cafaggio 1988   13   £D
A velvety mature beast.

Italian Table Wine (1 litre)   10   £C

Lungarotti Cabernet Sauvignon 1987   14   £C
Dry blackcurrant with a woody edge to it, smooth as silk.

Montepulciano d'Abruzzo 1991   13   £B

ITALIAN WINE – *white*

Bianco Veronese 1991   13   £B
Great value for such firm, clean, fruity drinking.

Chardonnay	13	£C
Frascati Superiore 1991	12	£C
Italian Table Wine (1 litre)	11	£B
Orvieto Superiore 1991	11	£B
Soave (1 litre)	10	£C

LEBANESE WINE – *red*

Hochar 1989   15 £D
There is no volatility from the usual grenache and syrah; just an effortlessly drinkable fruity wine of great length and flavour (logan and blackberries) but the whole effect is what is so attractive – it is truly wonderfully slip-downable, yet, at the same time, is distinctly Musar-like, yet younger and more supple.

NEW ZEALAND WINE – *white*

Chardonnay 1992   13 £C

Gisborne Dry White 1992   13 £C
A blend of muller-thurgau and sauvignon blanc from adolescent vines. Villa Maria will, if their other wines are anything to go by, eventually make this into a formidable wine in future vintages, I have a feeling.

Hawkes Bay Chardonnay 1991   12 £C
Some fresh-faced innocence here.

Marlborough Sauvignon Blanc 1991   14 £C
Typically herbaceous but finishing with a subtle touch of
honeyed fruit. Delicious.

Sauvignon Blanc 1992   13 £C

PORTUGUESE WINE – *white*

Vinho Verde   13 £B
A delicious, frivolous little tipple.

SOUTH AFRICAN WINE – *red*

Cape Country Pinotage 1989   12 £B
Leathery, boxy, some ripe fruit.

Stellenbosch Cabernet Sauvignon 1990   12 £C

Stellenbosch Merlot/Cabernet Sauvignon 1992 14 £C
Decent value for under four quid: a really rich and pene-
tratingly fruity wine of bite and purpose.

SOUTH AFRICAN WINE – *white*

Cape Country Chenin Blanc 1992   15 £B
Gets better and better. Controlled peardrop fruit (woolly-
coated), fine balancing acidity. Lovely, fruity wine of dash and
style. Terrific value.

Cape Country Colombard 1992 11 £B

Cape Country Sauvignon Blanc 1991 14 £B
There really is some style here for just over three quid.
Indeed, there are sancerres on sale at twice the price which
are only half as good. Grapefruit, gooseberry, citrus – they're
all there and nicely balanced.

Chenin Blanc 1992 13 £B

Colombard 1992 12 £B

Stellenbosch Chardonnay 1992 13 £C

SPANISH WINE – *red*

Rioja 1990 13 £B
A decent price for a decent rioja.

Spanish Dry Red (3 litres) 14 £E
A lot of very dry, very attractive plum/blackcurrant fruit.
Excellent value for adult orgies and annual meetings of the
Neighbourhood Watch.

Valencia Red 16 £B
An enigma. I rated it 11 upon opening, 14 after half an hour,
and 16 after six hours. What begins with a limp handshake of
dilute cherry from a distant planet ends with the firm, savoury
grip of well-textured blackcurrant and dry, burnt cherry. A
most remarkable and utterly delicious turnaround and only
recommendable to those with the patience to wait one quarter
of a day before touching the opened bottle.

SPANISH WINE – *white*

Marqués de Griñon Rueda 1990   15   £D
The delightfully poised flowery undertones to the excellent
fruit/acid balance together produce a wine of thirst-
quenching elegance.

Medium White (3 litres)   13   £E
Yes, it sweetly finishes but it is not out of touch completely
with its acidity and a glass makes a refreshing aperitif.

Valencia White   14   £B
Offers less aromatic presence, and hardly more of an chro-
matic one, than tap water upon pouring, but its flavour perks
up mightily with time and it tastes agreeably, if subtly, of ogen
melon with a dash of lemon. The wine exerts considerable
charm with its drinkability increasing exponentially, helped by
an unaggressive 10.5% of alcohol, and I soon found my bottle
empty and three stories of V. S. Pritchett digested. Quite how
it would have coped with spicier fare, like Elmore Leonard or
Amis *fils*, say, is open to question but, at £2.99 the bottle, it's
worth its rating and the attentions of anyone with a soft chair
and light reading to hand or lots of thirsts to quench.

USA WINE – *white*

Woodbridge, Robert Mondavi Chardonnay
1989   14   £D
There is spice to this peach of a wine, but also freshness and
fullness.

SPARKLING WINE/CHAMPAGNE

Blanc de Blancs Champagne	12	£G

Blanc de Noirs Champagne 13 £F

Blush Frizzante 11 £B

Cava 12 £D

Champagne Veuve de Medts 14 £G
This is a gorgeous experience, even one for which you have had to shell out nearly £14 (the same price as one of Marks' natty cotton shirts). Elegant, full yet dry, with a soothing acidity typical of champagne at its incomparable best.

Crémant d'Alsace 14 £E
This wine has always stood favourable comparison with champagne.

Crémant de Bourgogne 13 £D

Desroches Champagne 13 £F

Nicholas Feuillatté 1982 14 £G
Well, it's passed its 11-plus and M&S customers are wealthy enough to take it through the checkout, nestling beside the caviare in their baskets, even at its monstrous price of nigh on twenty quid.

St-Gall Champagne 1985 12 £G
Rich and very drinkable and at its best with smoked salmon.

Saumur Ladubay 14 £D
What a little corker! A gorgeous chenin/chardonnay blend of quite arrogant aplomb.

Sparkling Chardonnay	13	£D
Sparkling Medium Dry	12	£C
Sparkling Rosé	13	£C

An engaging little fizzer.

Morrisons

On Monday 19 October 1992 I tasted the first wine to be made from grapes gathered during that year's French harvest to be put on sale in a British supermarket. Good old Morrisons. They didn't hang about for one moment. They tasted a bargain, they ordered masses of it, and they stuck it on sale *toute suite*. The wine whizzed out of their 50 northern stores in no time. The wine was called Vin Primeur and it was from that area to the west and south of Perpignan known as the Vin de Pays des Pyrénées Orientales and thus I was treated to a natural and perfect quaffing weight of alcohol (11%), a pleasant soft fruitiness reminiscent of dilute cherry underpegged by a very subtle nuttiness, and a freshness and energy about the finish which soothed the throat and inspired demands for an immediate second, third, and fourth glass.

Morrisons, the supermarket chain named as the best performing company in the whole of the British Isles in a survey by the business magazine *Director*, was the supermarket first with the Vin Primeur and it sums up their whole no-nonsense approach to bringing their customers cheap, no-nonsense wines. The wine was packed in a very pretty painted bottle depicting a butterfly flitting over unidentifiable vegetation, it cost £2.49 and rated 15 points. It was most enjoyable lightly chilled and a great accompaniment to fish and chips or more robust dishes like *crapaud dans le trou*.

I tell you all this because at the time of putting this book to press the 1993 vintage of this wine was not yet off the vine let alone in the bottle and on the shelf. So be warned. There's no reason to suppose this year's wine won't be as big a beauty, and as big a bargain as last's, and so I thought I should tip you the wink early. Of course, it could already be gone by now, Morrisons' customers being what they are, but that's the chance you take in this business. On the other hand, the store may have given the wine a miss this year.

Goodness knows, there are plenty of other opportunities at Morrisons. The store breathes bargains from the wine shelves to the veg counter. As long as they don't try to move south and do business with us snooty southerners they'll carry on being a great place to spend your money.

ARGENTINIAN WINE – *red*

Trapiche Malbec   13   £C

AUSTRALIAN WINE – *red*

Coldridge Estate Shiraz/Cabernet Sauvignon   13   £B
Good value. A lighter style of shiraz blend which squeaks with fruit rather than screams.

Barramundi Shiraz/Merlot   14   £C
Sweaty, leathery, soft and fruity. Treat the turkey to it.

AUSTRALIAN WINE – *white*

Coldridge Estate Semillon/Chardonnay   13   £B

Hardy's Private Bin Chardonnay 1992   15   £B
Delightful summery feel to this wine with its pineapple and
apple acidity undercutting citric-edged melon fruit. Terrific
value.

CHILEAN WINE – *red*

Cousino-Macul Cabernet Sauvignon 1988   14   £C
Ripe, rich, satisfying. Soft as taffeta, with subtle tobacco hints
to the fruit.

Gato Negro Cabernet Sauvignon   12   £B

San Pedro Merlot   14   £C
Dark, rich, with well-developed fruit. A fine roast meat wine.

CHILEAN WINE – *white*

Chilean Sauvignon Blanc   13   £B

Gato Blanco Sauvignon Blanc   12   £B

FRENCH WINE – *red*

Beaujolais-Villages, H. Leger 1990   12   £C

Brouilly, Duboeuf   12   £D
See entry for Regnie.

Cellier la Chouf, Minervois 14 £A
Excellent value, softly tannic, friendly wine. Daft price.

Château Cantenac, Côtes de Bourg 1988 13 £C
A far from indecent bit of claret at a very decent price.

Corbières, Les Fenouillets 1992 14 £A
A genuine, and rare, sod-in-the-gob wine. Real dirt – it
literally tastes of the soil and it's handsome with burnt meats.
Let it breathe for two hours before attempting to swallow it.

Côtes du Rhône 1990 (Morrisons) 12 £B
Light but very drinkable.

Côtes du Rhône 1991 13 £B
A rhône from the quiet side of the river – but excellent value.

Côtes du Rhône Louis Bonnard 1991 10 £A

**Côtes du Rhône Villages, Claudine Epitalon
1992** 10 £B

Côtes du Ventoux, J. P. Léon 1991 13 £B
Smashing pasta wine. Very attractive soft fruit.

Fleurie, Duboeuf 12 £D
See entry for Regnie.

Fortant Cabernet Sauvignon 12 £B

Fronton 1989 13 £C

Ginestet Bordeaux 12 £B
Some typical bordeaux austerity detectable here.

La Rose St-Jean, Bordeaux (half) 14 £A
A simple light claret of great interest to solo lunchers in its
odd size. Good touch of soft fruit on the woodiness.

La Vieille Ferme, Côtes du Ventoux   13   £C

Le Vigneron Catalan   13   £B
Can't grumble at this much reasonable fruit for the money.
Also in magnums for under a fiver – useful party size.

Merlot, Vin de Pays d'Oc 1992   13   £B
Some softness here and attractive plummy fruity. Excellent
value.

Regnie, Duboeuf   12   £D
Regnie is the newest beaujolais cru name. It used to be plain
Beaujolais-Villages but it's been upgraded. But like seemingly
all beaujolais crus nowadays (Brouilly and Fleurie, for
example, also at Morrisons), or at least the cru wines which
find their way into British supermarkets, the same high 13%
of alcohol is offered along with the high price and though
these wines are smooth, sweetly fruity and reliable, and drinkable immediately upon opening (making them restaurant pro-
ducts really) as value for money they are beaten hollow by
cheaper reds from all over the world.

Vin de Pays des Bouches du Rhône   13   £B
You could chill this red and it would serve the same happy
end as a white (if you wore a blindfold as you drank it) but at
average room temperature, whatever that may mean, touches
of baked earth and herbs on the fruit are apparent which make
it the sort of thing you find in Marseille transport cafés as the
vin rouge de maison. As you knock it back you sense the
proximity of mountaineous off-white vested Frogmen with
oil-stained fingers and yellow cigarettes dangling from their
lips. Having said that, though, the wine has an interesting
soiled nappy aroma. Not a wine I'd try offering mothers, child
minders, nannies, paediatricians, or men under seventy-five
years of age. Looks like grandpa's stuck with it then (and he'll

be thrilled with it if he sucks it up through his shag-packed pipe).

| Vin de Pays des Coteaux de l'Ardèche | 12 | £A |

| Vin de Pays des Pyrénées Orientales | 15 | £B |

It should go on sale just as this book does – pipping the bubble-gummy nouveau from Beaujolais by a week or so. And it pips that overrated fruit juice in other departments: it's cheaper, fruitier and fresher, and less alcoholic. A great start to the winter season (if Morrisons stock it like the store did last year).

FRENCH WINE – *white and rosé*

| Cépage Muscat, Pyrénées Orientales 1990 | 13 | £B |

| Chablis, Paul Tourier 1992 | 11 | £C |

| Chais Baumière Chardonnay | 14 | £C |

One of the classiest and best chardonnays made in the south of France.

| Côtes de Provence Rosé 1992 | 8 | £B |

| Côtes de Duras Sauvignon Blanc 1992 | 14 | £B |

Fine level of fruit, cleanly finished. Something of a bargain.

| Côtes du Rhône | 12 | £B |

| Côtes du Roussillon Blanc de Blancs | 10 | £B |

| Foncaussade, Côtes de Bergerac Moelleux 1991 | 9 | £B |

| J. P. Chenet, Cinsaut Rosé 1992 | 10 | £B |

An amusing wine: the back label tells us 'to be drunk to any dish', and the bottle itself is drunk – or rather it was produced by a conspicuously inebriated bottle maker who likes to stick his neck out and then bend it. These unflattering clues should be sufficient to tell us the kind of wine within.

Jalibert Bergerac Sec	10	£B
Le Vigneron Catalan	10	£A

Le Vigneron Catalan Rosé1991   12   £A
Would best show off its charms, I believe, swigged in July under a Côte d'Azur plane tree along with a whopping salad niçoise, but in Britain in winter, however clement, it's hard pushed to rate much more than 12 points with a tuna sandwich for company.

Muscadet, La Sablière 1992	10	£C
Pinot Blanc Victor Preiss	12	£C
Vin de Pays des Coteaux de l'Ardèche 1992	11	£A
Vin de Pays des Côtes de Thau	13	£B

Vin de Pays des Côtes de Gascogne, Pouy 1992   12   £B
Rather good with live shellfish.

Vin de Pays du Jardin de la France 1992	6	£B

GERMAN WINE – *white*

Flonheimer Adelberg 1991   13   £A
Light, flimsy and bordering on the delicious.

Herxheimer Herrlich Kabinett   13   £B

Klusserather St. Michael 10 £B

St Johanner Abtey Ortega Spätlese 1992 12 £B
A drier, cheaper, and more complex alternative to lousy liebfraumilch.

Shellfish Dry 13 £B
Never was a wine as aptly named or priced.

Wehlener Klosterberg Kabinett 1991 12 £C
An amusing aperitif. Doesn't pack a lot of punch but it does
have a tasty tart level of fruit and tongue-prickling acidity.

Wiltinger Scharzberg Spätlese 13 £B

GREEK WINE – *red*

Mavrodaphne of Patras 10 £B
This is a basically stewed prunes made into wine. Probably
rather good with Christmas pudding.

HUNGARIAN WINE – *red*

Cabernet Sauvignon 1991 11 £B
Not as spinelessly fruity as its weedy pong might suggest.

Country Wine 14 £A
Lies as soft and as comforting on the tongue as a pillow.

Merlot, Szekszard Region 1992 12 £B
Good sausage and mash wine.

HUNGARIAN WINE – *white*

Chardonnay 1992   14   £B
A spirited attempt to reach a rich level of fruit surprising for
the money. A very attractively contrived wine to swig by itself
rather than to dwell on and muse about for its varietal values.

Country Wine   12   £A
A light muscat style wine as frivolous as a snowflake.

Sauvignon Blanc 1992   14   £B
Brilliant, clean, crisp fish wine. Like old-style muscadet
ordinaire.

ITALIAN WINE – *red*

Barolo Fontanafredda   12   £E

Gabbia d'Oro   8   £A
Are you prepared for the extravagant experience which follows shelling out all of two quid (+9p) for this wine?

Merlot, Grave del Friuli 1992   12   £A
Soft, light, very pleasant.

Montepulciano d'Abruzzo   13   £B
Good value. Dry and cheerful.

Sangiovese di Romagna   13   £B

Tonino   10   £B
A crumbly cherry biscuit wine of little character but some
imbecilic charm. Tonino was first created as a brand for

Seagrams over 20 years ago by a half-baked advertising copy-writer who loved wine. Poor chap lost his marbles some years after this and became a wine writer. Do not ask me how I know these things.

Valpolicella (Morrisons)	12	£B

ITALIAN WINE – *white*

Del Colle, Veneto, Chardonnay	13	£C
Est! Est!! Est!!! Canaletto 1992	12	£B
Frascati Superiore Orsola 1992	10	£B
Orvieto Classico, Bigi	12	£C
Trebbiano del Veneto	10	£B
Trebbiano del Veneto, Pasqua 1992	10	£A

MEXICAN WINE – *red*

L.A. Cetto Cabernet Sauvignon	14	£C

Eat your hearts out, minor Bordeaux growths at three times the price.

PORTUGUESE WINE – *red*

Borges Bairrada Reserva 1987   14   £B
Good, rich, mature tone to the fruit without being strident or
brassy. Remarkable value.

Soveral   14   £A
Still amazing value for just over two quid.

PORTUGUESE WINE – *white and rosé*

Lezíria rosé   13   £A
Earthy aroma, roses and cherry fruit, prickly on the tongue.
Finishes with a nutty dryness. Difficult (no, impossible) to
find a tastier under-two-quid rosé.

Portuguese rosé   12   £B

Vinho Verde   12   £B

ROMANIAN WINE – *red*

Cabernet Sauvignon Reserve 1985   16   £B
For lunch one Sunday I decanted this 16-point wine and
served it to a well-heeled American wine buff and he was
bowled over by its lovely dry, dusty aroma and fruit and he was
touched that I had opened some ancient fifth growth claret
specially for him. When I revealed its true provenance and
stunning under-three-quid price tag, he admitted he would

have been less surprised to learn that Sylvester Stallone was dating Margaret Thatcher.

Merlot Special Reserve 1981 15 £B
Rich, powerful, forcefully mature wine needing rich and powerful playmates like marinated beef stew with carrots and wood mushrooms.

ROMANIAN WINE – *white*

Sauvignon Blanc 12 £B

SOUTH AFRICAN WINE – *red*

Cinsault 1992 14 £B
This is so thick, soft and creamy with fruit that it reminds me of the cherry blossom boot polish I used on my school shoes. A real forwardly fruity number of superb relevance when tomato-sauced pizzas and pastas are on the table. It almost hums with velvet berries.

Culemborg pinotage 12 £B

SOUTH AFRICAN WINE – *white*

Cape Country Chenin Blanc 13 £B

SPANISH WINE – *red*

Campo Viejo Reserva	13	£D

Campo Viejo Rioja 13 £C

A reliable dollop of woody fruit. I've only once sent a bottle of this wine back and it was in a tapas bar in Madrid but the bottle was twenty years old, had been badly stored, and even the bloke behind the bar spat it out when he tasted it. He graciously presented me with a younger bottle – perhaps catching the sound of quaking English feet in boots amidst the deathly silence which instantaneously fell on the crowded bar as I handed the bottle back. But with this bottle, you should have no complaints.

Marqués de Cáceres Rioja 13 £C

Raimat Abadia 14 £D

Classy and distinguished.

Rioja 1991 15 £B

One of the under-three-quid marvels of Rioja. Lush, soft, vanilla fruit. Gloriously light and tingling and almost quixotic in its desire to please.

Torres Sangredetoro Tres Torres 1989 14 £C

This has some pretensions to be much finer than it is, not helped by the plastic bull dangling from the neck like some cornflake packet give-away gee-gaw, for it has satiny fruit of some depth and class and as a wine for poultry dishes it is excellent. Under £4 it's also well-priced but somehow the feeling grows, as does the ullage as the wine slips down the throat, that there's passion missing, along with the customary vividly orchestrated fruit we've come to expect from Señor Torres.

SPANISH WINE – *white*

Deliciosa Manzanilla   15   £D
Nutty and saline. At its best with almonds or pistachios as an
aperitif or smoked ham. Absurdly cheap for such aristrocratic
classy wine.

Inocente Extra Dry Fino   16   £D
Sherry, yes, but so dry it puckers your cheeks. Fabulously
satisfying when it's well chilled and taken with grilled prawns.
The mineral, flinty fruit tiptoes on the tongue like a ballet
dancer on shoes spun from cobwebs. Remarkable value.

La Mora, Moscatel de Valencia   15   £B
Great fun! Liquid raisins laced with nougat ice-cream.

Spanish Dry (Morrisons)   13   £A
Great value for large groups.

USA WINE – *red*

Blossom Hill   11   £B
Stale pot pourri aroma, sweet fruit. Might make an interesting
jelly with a game dish.

Glen Ellen Merlot 1990   16   £C
The universe's most perfect roast chicken wine in a bottle
labelled like a cross between golden shag pipe tobacco and
malt whisky. But this at least has the virtue of keeping sales
down and thus the price. Comes from a family-managed
vineyard in California (perfect for a family-managed store like
Morrisons) and its arresting cedary aroma leads to a soft, dry

fruit with a dark cherry-liqueur edge to its general earthiness
and it goes magnificently with a plain roast chicken – a
flavoursome beast, mind, not one that's been barred from
sowing a few wild oats.

USA WINE – *white*

Blossom Hill	11	£B

SPARKLING WINE/CHAMPAGNE

Asti Spumante   10   £C
A small glass with banana cake might do.

Moscato Spumante   11   £B
Shaving foam in a glass.

Nicole d'Aurigny champagne   16   £E
Good to see that Oz and Jilly read this book last year and
discovered this magnificently rich deep sparkler for the
BBC's Food & Drink programme.

Omar Khayyam, India   12   £D

Paul Herard Brut champagne   13   £F

Paul Herard Demi-Sec Champagne   12   £F

Schloss Bochingen   10   £C

Seaview Brut 15 £C
One of the best sparklers on the market under £5: stylish, refined.

Vouvray (Morrisons) 14 £D
Good value sparkler.

Safeway

Considering the sympathetic prices of many of Safeway's wines, The Ladies Home for Gentlewomen of Small Means in London's famous Abbey Road is the most appropriate place for the store's spring wine tasting but instead it holds the occasion, and has done for some years past, at the University Women's Club, a welcoming establishment situated in the tart-bestrewn streets of Mayfair. The Club is quite easily the pleasantest venue for a wine tasting in London, for the bottles to be tasted take up the whole wooded library, the fully stocked shelves excepted, and a good deal of the deliberative taster's time is spent wondering how well the wines he is enjoying might go with the original edition Woolfs, Plaths and Sparks ranged about him. Would, I wonder, the *Selected Letters of Philip Larkin*, a book which had me holding my sides in mirth many times, find a place amidst this bastion of intelligent femininity? I know the Safeway wine to go with Larkin. It is La Coume de Peyre 1992, for it is ripe and melon-bright, outspokenly fruity, excellent value for money and great by itself. It is a white Vin de Pays des Côtes de Gascogne, rates 15 points, and it costs £3.29.

This is only one of many attractive Safeway wines I have taken out of the library and put in this book. Many others, many of the most interesting, come from eastern Europe. The store's Young Vatted wines from Bulgaria are a terrific initiative and they've brought back from their Hungarian travels some extremely attractive wines. I discovered for myself how fertile, imaginative and wide-ranging is the Hungarian wine scene when earlier this year I went there myself and saw the Safeway wine buyers in action.

I found Hungary a fascinating and a baffling place. Take the language. Ask the bloke standing next to you in the bus queue if he knows the Hungarian word for 'woman' and he will come back at you with the correct answer every time. On this basis you might think Hungarian a pushover to learn. It is not. I always like to able to say at least 'good morning' and 'thank you' in the language of any country I visit but Hungarian had me gasping. A language in which *no* means 'woman' (and *bor* is 'wine') had me floored. So here I am in Kiskoros, a town on the great plain between the Dunube and Tisza rivers, staring at Marta Domokos, a five-foot-nothing Hungarian *no* winemaker, and I want very much to tell her personally that her wines make the world a better place but I have to rely on an interpreter to do this for me. The fact that I am in the same boat (*ugyanugy elkuld*, in case you wondered) as the Safeway wine buyers brings me little comfort.

As it happened, my unalloyed delight at her '92 vintage wines was obvious and unmasked. She blushed. I strongly suspected that the Safeway buyers liked the wines too but, perversely, it's to their advantage they had no more fluency in Hungarian than did I; for they're the ones with the money to spend and one of the things I've learned from watching supermarket buyers at work is that they operate like poker players. They never let the guys round the table know what they're really thinking and they like to bet on certs. The fewer words spoken the better. The wines, in the final analysis, speak for everyone.

Therefore, for the outrageous sum of £2.59 you can acquire one of Marta Domokos' red wines metamorphosed from a 100 per cent kekfrancos grape variety wine in the tasting room to a niftily labelled Safeway Hungarian Country Wine 1992 on the shelf. It is an absolute 15-point lip-smackin' bargain. Nicely alcoholic at around 11.5%, alive and wriggling with young rounded fruit like some beaujolais of yesteryear, it has immense charm. Fresh with plummy fruit, with touches of smoke and rubber and a natural fruity finish of toffeed figs, it is delicious gently chilled by itself, or shared in the sun in the park at lunchtime with bread and cheese, or knocked back with an evening meal of anything from pasta to pizza or even a posh seduction do with only two places at table and candlelight between.

In situations such as the last you might need a white wine to kindle an appetizing spark and the Domokos/Safeway team has the perfect inflammatory answer with Chardonnay 1992. Again, it's wickedly cheap at £2.85 and well deserving of its 15 points for it has elegantly subtle touches of rich butter with a bitter almond finish. Old-fashioned in style and structure including the price, and heartening to drink without food or to accompany salads, fish, chicken and vegetable dishes. It was touching to see Marta's delight at my nakedly enthusiastic appreciation of it.

I must say I think Safeway missed a trick not asking me to come up with the names for these wines. Hungarian Country Wine and Chardonnay 1992 don't sound half so intriguing as SuperMarta's Great Plain Plonks. However, I was pleased to be instrumental in persuading the buyers to consider the BB Sparkling Brut we found frothing away in our glasses at one tasting. I have a strong suspicion that this wine would have been ignored, as it had been by other supermarket buyers who tasted it before we did, had I not banged the table. At £3.99, this peachy bubbly is a 15-point winner.

However, even with wines like these, adding to an already burgeoning reputation for innovation among wine drinkers and wine writers, I was surprised to find the nation's most polished literary reviewer and wine lyricist, Mr Auberon Waugh, in the Women's University Library. He told me he was there to find out if all the pats on the shoulder Safeway wines were getting were deserved. Later, when this aristocrat of literary editing, with his knowledgeable palate, recommended some Safeway wines to his *Spectator* readers I was forced to speculate that the next thing we'll be seeing is Her Majesty and Phil pushing a trolley down the Safeway aisles, arguing over which bottle will go best with the roast Welsh lamb for Charlie's birthday. Hopefully, they'll have a copy of this book to hand. And Faber can stick a Royal Appointment badge on the front cover.

ARGENTINIAN WINE – *red*

Carrascal 1985   13   £D
Goodness, what a serious, austere, almost monkish wine was to be tasted in this bottle in the spring. By winter it may have a soft smile on its face.

Caso del Campo syrah 1992   10   £C

AUSTRALIAN WINE – *red*

Cabernet Sauvignon 1992   14   £B
What a blackcurrant smoothie! With a glug of it in one cheek and a morsel of roast lamb or beef in the other you'll be seriously satisfied.

Coldstream Hills Pinot Noir 1989   13   £E

Hardys Nottage Hill Cabernet Sauvignon 1990   14   £C
A sneaky cough-sweetness lurks within the folds of this
yummy, value for money specimen, making it a must for anyone
with swollen tonsils but not a swollen wallet.

Jacob's Creek Dry Red 1990   13   £C

Orlando RF Cabernet Sauvignon 1989   13   £C

Penfolds Bin No. 2 Shiraz/Mataro 1991   14   £C

Penfolds Cabernet Sauvignon Coonawarra
1989   14   £E
The word *coonawarra* derives from the aboriginal for
honeysuckle but it is not honey which its extraordinary rust red
soil suckles best but long-living red wines, and they can be the
finest shirazes and cabernets in Australia. This wine offers us a
clue to its excellence with its stunningly deep colour, and dry,
teeth-rattling fruit. I dare say it might repay cellaring for a few
years (though this is not one of those Coonawarras which
legendarily reach their peak after three decades) but it is
superbly drinkable now and certainly with rich cheeses.

Penfolds Koonunga Hill Shiraz/Cabernet 1990   14   £C
Big, tub-thumping figgy fruit. Great panache.

Rosemount Cabernet Sauvignon 1989   13   £D

Shiraz (Safeway)   14   £B
One of Safeway's competitors tried to hoodwink me into
buying the idea that this soft, modern, eminently gluggable
wine, which travels in bulk from Australia to France to be
bottled and bagged-in-box before crossing the Channel to fill
Safeway's shelves, wasn't good enough for *his* store. Poppy-
cock. Pure jealousy. This is a smashing little wine at a smashing
little price and who gives a kookaburra's fart if it makes
corkscrews redundant?

Taltarni Cabernet Sauvignon 1989   13   £E
I'd open this wine in 2005. And then the men in black coats
can cart me away and chisel on my tombstone: *He led a full,
rich life.*

The Magill Estate 1988   13   £F
Tremendous stuff. But wait.

Tyrrells Old Winery Pinot Noir 1991   10   £D
A sweet copy of a burgundy.

**Wolf Blass Yellow Label Cabernet Sauvignon
1988**   13   £D

AUSTRALIAN WINE – *white*

Australian Chardonnay 1992   12   £C
Attractive rubbery fruit but not quite enough balancing acidity
to make it outstanding.

Cru Australis Sauvignon Blanc 1992   12   £A

Eileen Hardy Selection Chardonnay 1988   10   £F

Evans & Tate Two Vineyards Chardonnay 1992   14   £E
Well-developed, supple fruit rippling with muscles – a sort of
Chippendale of a wine without being such a soppy show-off.

Hardy Gewürtztraminer/Riesling 1991   15   £C
This has a wonderful daft charm, with its spicy toffee aroma
and tickle of sherbet lemon on the vivid splash of fruit, and,
curiously, it is dry. An aperitif or for drinking with light
oriental food.

| Jacob's Creek Semillon/Chardonnay 1991 | 13 | £C |

| Orlando RF Chardonnay 1990 | 13 | £C |

Plantagenet Muscat Bindoon 1990 13 £D
Great sweet citric aperitif or dessert wine with fresh apples or
pears.

| Rosemount Chardonnay, Oak-Matured 1990 | 13 | £D |

Rosemount Roxburgh Chardonnay 1991 16 £G
Gorgeous golden colour. Fine, complex, outstanding, deeply
committed wine with a traditional gaminess to the fabulous
fruit. Only the brightness of this aromatic fruit as it reaches
the tongue tells you this is Aussie chardonnay and not a
product of some venerable vineyard of the Côte d'Or. It is
massively expensive, the price of a pair of decent trousers at
BHS, but many a drinker might go trouserless given the
choice.

Rosemount Show Reserve 1990 14 £E
Splendiferous fruit-laden wine for chardonnay lovers who
appreciate a touch of exotica to their favourite grape. A gorgeous mouthful of rich, well-made wine.

| Semillon (Safeway) | 12 | £B |

| Semillon/Chardonnay 1992 (Safeway) | 12 | £C |

**Wolf Blass Oak-Matured Chardonnay,
Bilyara 1989** 13 £D

AUSTRIAN WINE – *white*

Lenz Moser Pinot Blanc 1991   15   £C
Delicious dry, fruity wine, with a graceful introduction via a
toasty aroma through to a clean finish. A balanced, elegantly
structured wine at a bargain price.

Seewinkler Impressionen Ausbruch 1991 (half)   13   £D
A burnt-honey edge to the fruit which is aromatically attractive. Has some botrytis character (i.e. the true noble rot fungus
has set into the grapes thus dehydrating them and enriching
the fruit), but this is not hugely concentrated and you pay
through the nose for it.

BULGARIAN WINE – *red*

Cabernet Sauvignon 1988   15   £B
Remarkable price for a five-year-old and delicious stuff it is.
Wonderful woody perfume, but not a trace of arthritic fruit,
just supple, cherry-cheeked, figgy richness.

**Bulgarian Country Wine Pinot/Merlot
(Safeway)**   13   £B

**Cabernet Sauvignon Suhindol (Safeway)
(3 litres)**   13   £F

Mavrud 1992   13   £B

Merlot Reserve 1987   14   £B
Scrumptious wine of lush plum and blackberry fruit.
Balanced, dry, very well made.

Young Vatted Merlot and Young Vatted
Cabernet Sauvignon 1992   15 £B

Personally, I like my wines without Vat if I can get them, but
here we are with two wines proudly proclaiming their vat-
tedness to the complete mystification of the customer. The
reason for their name lies in the fact that these wines, being
unlike other red Bulgars which habitually spend time ageing
in oak barrels, have been bottled from the vat. But what really
sets them apart is their depth of fruit, their freshness and
flavour, and their overall style, which is a result of their
manner of fermentation – the so-called carbonic maceration
method made famous in Beaujolais in which no crushing
takes place but instead the whole berries are allowed to fer-
ment as a mass pressed by their own weight. These are two
tremendous wines for under £3 the bottle each. Both exhibit
varietal fidelity, both are brilliantly put together. The merlot
has a polished unguency and swirling depth of flavour which
went beautifully with the goat's cheese and bread I ate with it,
whilst the blackcurranty cabernet is more savoury and will do
any roast or stew proud. Both represent the very opposite of
taxing tippling.

BULGARIAN WINE – *white*

Bulgarian Country Wine (Safeway)   12 £A

CHILEAN WINE – *red*

Don Maximiano Cabernet Sauvignon 1988　　14　£D
Extraordinary aroma of herbs, mint and violets, but the fruit's
all in one piece and the finish is soft.

San Pedro Cabernet Sauvignon 1992　　14　£B
Soft, attractive, plummy fruit – leathery undertones. Delicious
and very good value.

Santa Rita Medalla Real 1989　　15　£D
Not cheap but a gorgeous, dry wine with blackcurrant fruit
and a sweet rich finish. Soft, sustaining – and of huge appeal
to meat stew eaters.

Villa Montes Cabernet Sauvignon 1990　　13　£C
Very attractive pasta plonk.

CHILEAN WINE – *white*

Caliterra Sauvignon Blanc 1991　　15　£B
One of the classiest sauvignon blancs on sale under £4.

Domaine Oriental Sauvignon/Semillon 1992　　11　£C

**Santa Carolina Special Reserva Chardonnay
1992**　　15　£D
This is a big, chewy old-style wine of great character. Oily and
polished on the tongue, it has a lovely weight of fruit without
being blowzy. I drank a bottle with a baked fish smothered in
salsa verde sauce (capers and anchovies in it, no less) and it
coped splendidly – in circumstances in which many a

European chardonnay would have been forced to run up the white flag.

CYPRIOT WINE – *red*

Ambelida 1991   12   £C

CZECH WINE – *white*

Pinot Blanc 1992   15   £B
In my experience, no supermarket, or high street wine shop
for that matter, has yet managed to drag any heart-warming
vinous treasures back from the vineyards of what was once
Czechoslavakia – with the exception of this wine. It comes
from a winery in Moravia (with winemakers furiously keen to
improve after years of communist indifference and a commercial manager who once worked for Marks & Spencer) and it's
rich and herby with an interesting maturity of fruit of great
individuality. Excellent with chicken and rich fish dishes.

ENGLISH WINE – *white*

Cinque Port Classic 1990   14   £C
One of the most enjoyable of the genre.

Denbies Surrey Gold 1990   13   £D
Good vegetal touches, plus honey on the fruit. One of the

craftiest English wines I've tried – by which I mean it can craftily fool the taster in the tasting room into giving it a higher rating than it deserves, for when it's drunk with food, or by itself, the sweetness on the finish jars. It has too much residual sugar for my liking, perhaps an attempt by its makers to ape New World brassy fruitiness, and what smells and swills like an outstanding wine has, going down the throat, not enough balancing acidity to bring you thirstily back for a fresh glass. Pity, for the vineyard would appear to produce fruit of a quality high enough to make first-class wine. At over a fiver, the drinker who will best appreciate Surrey Gold would, I think, prefer less gold and more silver.

Elmham Park 1990	11	£D
Like a muted liebfraumilch.		
Estate Selection Dry, Sharpham 1990	13	£C
Reasonable delivery of fresh fruit, sane and balanced.		
Lymington Medium Dry 1990	11	£C
Like a muted Elmham Park 1990.		
Pilton Manor Dry Reserve 1990	13	£C
Delicious. In the muscadet mould.		
Regatta, Valley Vineyards 1991	13	£C
Keen, fresh, dry – a grilled sardine wine.		
Stanlake 1992	13	£C
Sussex Reserve 1990	12	£C
Excellent with shellfish.		
Tenterden Special Reserve 1989	10	£D
Three Choirs Seyval Reichensteiner 1990	14	£C
Apple-bright fruit, developed and attractive, wrapped in wet		

wool i.e. that musty feral aroma given off by a sodden sweater drying in front of the fire. A dry wine of great style.

Valley Vineyards Dry White 1990   13   £C
14 grape varieties go to make this very creditable stab at a damn good white wine which only fails to impress at the finish. Until then it is fragrant and lush.

Wickham Vintage Selection 1990   13   £C
An off-dry wine in which the appley fruit is boosted by sucrose on the finish and tastes all the better for it. Good aperitif.

FRENCH WINE – *red*

Abbaye de Tholomies, Minervois 1989   15   £B
Terrific value for such dry, well-muscled fruit. Supple, athletic, delicious.

Beaujolais (Safeway)	11	£C
Beaujolais-Villages 1991 (Safeway)	12	£C
Beaune Luc Javelot 1989 (Safeway)	12	£D
Bourgogne Oak-Aged 1990 (Safeway)	10	£D
Brouilly, Duboeuf 1991	12	£D

**Cabernet Sauvignon, Oak-Aged Vin de Pays
d'Oc 1991 (Safeway)**   13   £C

Cairanne, Côtes du Rhône Villages 1990   13   £C
Good value for a good CdR.

Carruades de Lafite 1987 12 £F

Possibly, *possibly*, might acquire some character some time in the first quarter of the next century.

Château Baratet 1990 13 £C

An organic bordeaux which is blackcurranty and has an eager softness.

Château Biston Brillette, Moulis 1989 13 £E

Very attractive, well-made wine but somewhat numb in the fruit department when tasted in the spring (though this château and its regional *appellation* make traditionally forward clarets which can be drunk young). But I think it will improve considerably over a year or more and, though not cheap and suffering from severe competition from the Australians who cram twice this wine's fruit into a bottle for half the money, it might well emerge a real stylish number.

Château Brondelle, Graves 1989 12 £C

Château Canteloup, Médoc 1989 12 £C

Château Castera 1990 12 £C

This château can turn some of the best value bordeaux on the market. But it does need a little time to develop the woody fruitiness that is its hallmark.

Château de Caraguilhes, Corbières 1989/90 14 £C

I've always liked the way the wines from this organic estate taste like they were grown in good rich red earth, in which herbs and pine trees grow, and not put together by pale-faced white-coated chemists in laboratories. But then I'm an incurable romantic.

Château Duluc, St-Julien 1989 13 £E

Château Haut-Bages Averous, Pauillac 1985   12   £G

Château Joanny, Côtes du Rhône 1991   13   £B
Soft-hearted brute.

Château Kirwan, Margaux 1987   12   £E

Château La Lagune, Haut-Mèdoc 1987   13   £F
Needs time to develop the fullness and gracious richness this
Médoc classically displays but, even so, you can drink it now.
It will only poison your wallet.

Château La Salle Poujeaux, Haut-Médoc 1985   11   £E

Château La Tour de Mons, Margaux 1988   11   £E

Château Laroze, St-Emilion 1986   14   £E
Classic. Impressive. A lovely herby, woody, supple wine.

**Château Ludon Pomies Agassac,
Haut-Médoc 1988**   10   £D

Château Mendoce, Côtes de Bourg 1990   15   £C
Amazing the difference a year makes: this '90 scores 50 per
cent better than the '89 and not surprisingly for the new
vintage is a lovely woody, herby, classically fruity organic wine
with layers of blackcurrant fruit of dryness and softness plus a
subtle nuttiness. I especially like the organic photo of the
château on the label. (NB: the photographer is also available
for weddings and children's parties.)

Château Plantey, Pauillac 1988   11   £E

Château Puy Barbe, Côtes de Bourg 1989   13   £C

Château Tour de Beaupoil 1990   12   £C

Châteauneuf-du-Pape, La Source aux Nymphes 1989 13 £D
A saucy name for a saucy wine with a saucy price.

Claret Oak-Aged 1990 (Safeway) 14 £C
Superb, mature, woody fruit aromas and flavours. Good fruit and another claret lovers' bargain.

Corbières (Safeway) 11 £B

Côtes du Rhône (Safeway) 12 £B

Côtes du Roussillon Villages 1988 (Safeway) 12 £B

Côtes du Ventoux (Safeway) 11 £B

Domaine Anthéa, Merlot, Vin de Pays d'Oc 1991 13 £B
An organic merlot of extraordinarily good value for money: dry and softly earthy. And it improves quickly in bottle. Indeed, it comes out of the vat unworldly and semi-literate and after a year in bottle it's tri-lingual and an expert on cosmic strings.

Domaine Barret, Crozes-Hermitage 1991 14 £D
Like putting your nose into a ham sandwich. Delicious, raspberry-tinged plum fruit – dry yet vivid. A lush syrah beauty and a great beef stew wine.

Domaine de l'Amérique, Costières de Nîmes 1991 13 £B

Domaine de Soulie 1991 13 £C
An organic St-Chinian which is packed with mouth-filling plummy fruit with a good zing to it.

Domaine la Tuque Bel-Air, Côtes de Castillon 1988 14 £C
Great fruit punch of blackcurrants and damsons.

Domaine Richeaume, Cabernet Sauvignon
1989   15   £E
The '90, now coming through on the shelves, I was unable to
taste, but this '89, of which there may be odd bottles still
available, is an absolute stunner.

French Organic Vin de Table (Safeway)   11   £B

Les Hautes Restanques, Gigondas 1991   12   £D

Margaux, Barton & Guestier 1989   11   £E

Médoc 1991   14   £C
Grassy, merlot-like aromas and rather austere, but with roast
lamb and suchlike, it finds its feet and the fruit is most
attractive. An interesting blend of two châteaux wines; a
marriage arranged specially for Safeway. Claret lovers will
find this wine a bargain.

Merlot 1992, Vin de Pays des Coteaux
de l'Ardèche   12   £B

Minervois (Safeway)   12   £A

Pauillac, Club des Sommeliers 1988   10   £E

Prieuré Chateau Les Palais, Corbières 1991   13   £C
Blackberry jam spread.

St-Emilion Gabriel Corcol 1990   14   £C
Warm, attractive, and very good value for this classic style.

St-Julien, Barton & Guestier 1989   12   £E

Syrah, Vin de Pays des Coteaux de l'Ardèche,
(Safeway) (3 litres)   12   £B

Vin de Pays de l'Ardèche 1992 (Safeway)   12   £A

Vin de Pays de Vaucluse 1991   13   £A

Vin Rouge, Vin de Pays Catalan (Safeway)   10   £B

FRENCH WINE – *white and rosé*

Bergerac Sauvignon 1991 (Safeway)   13   £B
Good value.

Blanc de Bordeaux, Oak-Aged 1991   14   £C
Well-weighted fruit, good balance, excellent value.

Blaye Blanc 1992   14   £B
Excellent value for a fresh and fruity, well-balanced wine of great style. Good with grilled fish.

Bordeaux Rosé 1992   13   £B
Delightful onion-skin colour, delicious fruit, attractive price.

Bourgogne Blanc, Oak-Aged 1990 (Safeway)   10   £D

Cabernet d'Anjou Rosé   11   £B

Chablis, Domaine Yvon Pautre 1991   11   £D

**Chardonnay, Vin de Pays des Coteaux de
l'Ardèche 1991 (Safeway)**   14   £C

Château Canet, Entre-Deux-Mers 1991   13   £C
Organic but not yet orgasmic. A great improvement on the '90 vintage, and edging towards the delicious.

**Château de la Botinière, Muscadet Sur Lie
1991**   13   £C

Château Joanny Rosé 1992   14   £B
Rosé either exhibits a maddening lack of fruit or an infuriating
degree of over-zealous acidity and as a result seems neither
fish nor fowl. However, I have made a discovery. It is fish. Or
rather it is salmon fish cakes. With a plate of these splendid
things to sing along with Château Joanny is terrific. Joanny is a
Côtes du Rhône with a portrait on its label of Sir Clement
Freud, or a person who looks like this noted father figure and
British Rail sandwich inventor, but this only adds to the wine's
charms. It has a happy balance of plummy fruit and keen
acidity and whilst I dare say it might go well with other things,
and at £3.49 it's not expensive to discover what, the fish cakes
will do for me.

Château La Garousse, Bordeaux 1991   13   £C
Good fresh fruit and good value.

Château Le Pesquey, Bordeaux 1992   14   £B
Balance and equanimity. Even a touch of elegance on the
finish. Lots of grown-up fruit and balancing acidity make this
a very stylish wine. Further evidence that Bordeaux whites are
getting better and better.

Corbières Blanc de Blancs 1990 (Safeway)   12   £B

Côte de Beaune, Masey-Perier 1991   12   £D

Côtes du Luberon, Hugh Ryman 1992   13   £B
Very well made. Very good value.

**Domaine de Rivoyre Chardonnay, Vin de Pays
d'Oc 1991**   14   £C
Utterly delicious: dry, authoritative, demurely fruity and
balanced. Sounds like the perfect parliamentarian.

Domaine du Bosc, Vin de Pays des Coteaux d'Enserune 1992   14   £C
Rich, fresh, peachy wine of zest and kick.

Domaine Ste-Marie, Côtes du Rhône 1992   12   £C
Not as exciting as the '91 vintage because of the intrusion of the clairette grape variety in this previously 100 per cent bourboulenc curiosity.

Fortant de France Syrah Rosé, Vin de Pays d'Oc 1992   14   £C
Peardrops and cherry pastilles.

Gaillac 1992   11   £C

Gewürztraminer d'Alsace 1990 (Safeway)   14   £D

La Coume de Peyre 1992   15   £B
Ripe, melon-bright, outspokenly fruity, excellent value for money. An exceptional vin de pays des Côtes de Gascogne. For the correct reading matter to have to hand when drinking this wine, please refer to the introduction to this section.

Muscat, Cuvée José Sala   16   £C
Honeyed nougat on sweet raisin toast.

Pinot Blanc d'Alsace 1990   13   £C

Pouilly-Fumé, Les Cris 1992   12   £E
Has some delicious and haughty aspects but it's expensive. Only found in Safeways managed by ex-professional footballers who also have a grand master rating in chess.

Sancerre, Domaine de Petits Perriers 1991   12   £E
Pleasant with an interesting nutty finish.

Vin Blanc (Safeway)   10   £B

Vin de Pays d'Oc Sur Lie 1992   14   £B
Great value. Good fruit, freshly packed.

Vin de Pays de Vaucluse 1991   12   £A

**Viognier, Vin de Pays des Coteaux de
l'Ardèche 1992**   12   £C

Vouvray Demi-Sec   10   £C

GERMAN WINE – *red*

Dornfelder 1992   13   £C
A charming wine made by the charming Laubensteins, father
and daughter, and only its touch of expensiveness robs of it of
a higher rating (but then, talking to Herr Laubenstein, you
feel the pride of a man who, spiritually at least, has lovingly
picked, and his daughter trodden, every grape himself). This
is lushly fruity wine, a rebuke to faint hearts who say they can't
get along with red, and terrific with fried sausages, stuffed
roasts and grilled vegetables.

GERMAN WINE – *white*

Auslese 1988 (Safeway)   13   £C
Excellent aperitif to start the evening off.

**Bereich Bernkastel, Mosel-Saar-Ruwer
(Safeway)**   12   £B

**Dienheimer Tafelstein Scheurebe Kabinett
1991** 13 £C
Doktor Becker's interesting organic wine.

Gewürztraminer Rheinpfalz 13 £C
A model and inexpensive introduction to the grape but
experienced gewürzophiles may find it too undemanding.

Hock Deutscher Tafelwein (Safeway) 10 £A

Kabinett 1991 (Safeway) 12 £B

Leiwener Klostergarten Riesling Spätlese 1988 15 £C
Citric fruit, a slight touch of gunflint, elegant and mouth-
puckeringly delightful. Distinguished drinking for less than a
fiver.

Morio Muskat 1991, St Ursula 12 £B

Munsterer Rheinberg Riesling 1991 (50 cl) 14 £B
Utterly delightful wine for under £4 which is in a handy size
for a lone picnicker armed with ham sandwiches and a volume
of poetry.

Rulander Kabinett 1990 13 £C

**Ruppertsberger Nussbein Riesling Kabinett
1988** 14 £C
Under four quid for a wine of this quality? Unbelievable. An
attractive riesling aroma and fruit, keen and flinty yet rich and
fresh, and a good finish. Brilliant aperitif.

St Ursula Pinot Blanc 1990 11 £D

Spätlese 1990 (Safeway) 12 £B

Sylvaner Trocken 1991   14   £B
Lovely woody, herby aroma, and good fruit. Excellent value
for money.

GREEK WINE – *red*

Xinomavro Naoussis 1990   14   £C
A tongue twister. But with its dry blackcurrant and raspberry
fruit it's also a palate smoother and that's all that matters.

HUNGARIAN WINE – *red*

Cabernet Sauvignon Villany 1991   13   £B
Excellent value. A balanced, finely textured wine of good
fruity style.

Country Wine 1992   15   £B
A lip-smackin' bargain – see introduction to this section.

Estate Wine Merlot 1992   14   £C
An extremely pleasant, youthfully fruity wine from the Bat-
aapati winery, which is owned by the Antinori wine family of
Chianti fame.

Great Plain Kekfrancos 1992   13   £B

Merlot Villany 1991 (Safeway)   13   £A
Soft, fruity, attractive and very good value for money.

Reserve Cask F12 Cabernet Sauvignon 1991   14   £B
If this is the reserve cask what's the first choice like? Lafite

'45? The colour of this wine is like squashed sloes and blackberries, not much of an aroma, but a rich fruity flavour comes into the mouth intensely dry. With roast lamb, this is brilliant.

HUNGARIAN WINE – *white and rosé*

Cabernet Sauvignon Rosé 1992   15   £B
One of the driest yet most fruitily satisfying rosés for the money on sale.

Chardonnay 1992   15   £B
Elegantly subtle touches of butter with an almond finish. Marta Domokos of the Kiskoros winery, whose wine this is, may not fly like some winemakers in Hungary but she surely soars.

Country Wine 1992   15   £B
Bright, breezy, lovely balanced fruit – smashing aperitif tipple and brilliant value.

Dry Muscat Nagyrede   14   £B
Bit of a sharp finish cuts across the terrific muscat smell and taste and sure-footed dryness, but for all that great value for money. A first-rate aperitif.

Gyöngyös Chardonnay 1992   15   £B
As refreshing as a meadow after spring rain. Delicious, fresh, lemony chardonnay made in the modern way. Stainless steel finish.

Gyöngyös Estate Sauvignon Blanc 1992   14   £B
Lacks the pungency of the amazing '91 but still in fighting form and it's quite delicious.

Lake Balaton Chardonnay 1992   14   £B
Made by Nick Butler, flying Australian winemaker for the
Csopak winery near the shores of Europe's largest lake. Has a
nice fatty side to it, weighty fruit, good balance and some
freshness. Good with spicy fish dishes, I dare say.

Lake Balaton Pinot Gris 1992   15   £B
Another Nick Butler wine. This one makes a delicious aperitif, with its grass and buttercup richness.

Reserve Cask Olasz Riesling 1992   14   £B
A superb food wine, in spite of a woody aroma and a sourish
finish.

ISRAELI WINE – *red*

Carmel Cabernet Sauvignon   12   £C
An interesting curiosity; dry and respectably clothed in fruit.

ISRAELI WINE – *white*

Carmel Dry Muscat 1991   10   £B

Yarden Chardonnay 1991   13   £D
Highly drinkable, stylish, dry, well-made; expensive, but then
the Golan Heights can't be the easiest place in the world to
grow grapes.

ITALIAN WINE – *red*

Bardolino (Safeway)	13	£B
Chianti Classico 1890, Rocca delle Macie	13	£C
Chianti (Safeway)	12	£B

Don Giovanni 1990   14   £B

Surly but sexy. It comes from Sicily and is a blend of wines made from montelpulciano and nero d'avola grape varieties. Montepulciano is famous for adding its name and its juice to the wines of Abruzzo but its island fostering in this bottle has done it no harm except to be party to a wine which is somewhat drier and, ironically (considering the wine's eponym), not so immediately seductive as its northern cousin. This chewy, herby side to the wine is undoubtedly due to the addition of the nero d'avola which has been wood-aged. This wine is richly edged and full, will develop well in bottle over 1993 to get even softer and tastier and may well graduate to become a mega-magnificent 16-point Christmas luncheon wine. But this is pure speculation.

Lambrusco, Tenuta Generale Cialdini 1992   15   £B

Overshadowed by those millions of anonymous, sweet, fizzy bottles of feeble Italian blandness, could there lie a fresh, dry, pétillant *genuine* Lambrusco with an amazingly nutty fruitiness allied to a superbly swashbuckling acidity, together producing a 10.5% wine of great flavour and unique deliciousness? Yes, and here it is. This lambrusco oozes panache and style and it is worth any adventurous wine drinker's time and money. Drink the wine chilled, drink it with rich fish dishes, on its own, with a salad, or drink it with cold meats and salamis. But *drink it!!!*

Le Monferrine Dolcetto d'Asti 1992   12   £C

Montepulciano d'Abruzzo 1991   14   £B
Masses of swirling fruit in the mouth. Great stuff with pasta
dishes.

Salice Salentino Riserva 1986   12   £C
Rich and tarry, this wine a year ago dallied between savoury
fruit and a thrusting acid balance which together made for
great style and great taste and rated 15; however, it's getting to
the top of its particular hill right now and from being one of
the handsomest Italians in the store it is beginning to show a
few unwelcome wrinkles.

Sangiovese di Romagna   13   £B

Sicilian (Safeway)   14   £B
Terrific little plonk at a terrific little price.

Tenuta San Vito Chianti 1990   14   £C
Drier and more austere than is conventional with the type, but
then it says it's an organic wine, so that must be the reason.
Rather expensive for the type, too, but presumably the same
reason can be cited. But an excellent chianti for all that.

Valpolicella Classico 'Vigneti Marano' 1989   13   £C

Valpolicella (Safeway)   12   £B

ITALIAN WINE – *white*

Chardonnay del Triveneto 1991 (Safeway)   12   £C

I Frari, Bianco di Custoza 1991   13   £C
Great-looking bottle and delightfully chaotic labelling. No

points for this but certainly deserves 13 for its great degree of harmony and balance in the fruit/acid departments.

Le Monferrine, Chardonnay del Piemonte 1992 15 £C
This is astonishing value for the poshness of style on offer. A long, cool, elegant wine with top-drawer fruit. Attractive lemonic acidity.

Le Monferrine, Moscato d'Asti 1992 14 £B
5% alcohol but no mean sweet wine drunk with hard fruit.

Lugana 1991 13 £C
Pleasant lemony wine good with grilled chicken.

Orvieto Classico Secco 1990 (Safeway) 12 £B

Pinot Grigio del Triveneto 1991 (Safeway) 12 £B

Sicilian Dry 11 £B

Soave Classico, Monteleone 1990 14 £C
Lemons, nuts, and melons. What more could you ask of a real classico soave?

Soave (Safeway) 10 £B

Verdicchio delle Marche 1991 (Safeway) 12 £B

LEBANESE WINE – *red*

Château Musar 1985 15 £D
Exotic, hot, spicy, and getting softer and more attractive as it gets older. How nice if we all aged like that.

MOROCCAN WINE – *red*

Domaine Sapt Inour   15   £B
A kosher wine 'under strict control of grand rabbinat, Casablanca' which might more amusingly be called Rick's Place
Plonk or simply CasaRouge. It is an excellently put-together
wine of style and dash, blackcurranty and plummy, and I love
its unlikeliness and unabashed verve.

NEW ZEALAND WINE – *red*

Matua Valley Cabernet Sauvignon 1990   14   £E
Delicious with rare roast beef.

NEW ZEALAND WINE – *white*

Millton Vineyard Chardonnay 1992   13   £E
Attractive aperitif.

Millton Vineyard Sauvignon Blanc 1991   13   £E

Montana Chardonnay 1991 and 92   13   £C
Rich fruit in the '91 and the '92 is even friskier (and is
arguably tastier).

Montana Sauvignon Blanc 1992   14   £C
Marvellous new-mown grass aromas plus a lemon zestiness. It
feels like spring!

Taurau Valley 1992 15 £B
Lovely musty melon/lemon smell, delicious and inviting, with fruit to match. Great stuff and even better than the award-winning '91 vintage.

Wairu River Sauvignon Blanc 1992 14 £D
Lemon sherbet, grass and lime. This wine would whet a cow's appetite, let alone any ravenous human ruminant.

PORTUGUESE WINE – *red*

Bairrada 1988 (Safeway) 14 £C

Tinto da Anfora 1989 13 £D
Not as potently perfumed or as crushingly fruity as the great '88 vintage which had wine writers the length and breadth of the British Isles slavering – and fairly so. More acidity with this vintage and less warm fruit, but this is a function of its comparative youth and the wine will soften and tasty up. Apart from anything else Peter Bright, who makes this wine, couldn't turn out a duff bottle if he tried.

PORTUGUESE WINE – *white*

João Pires Muscat 1991 14 £C
Luscious, individual, powder-compact fresh fruit.

Lezíria 15 £A
This is a lovely, fresh wine at a terrific price. It has more attractive hay-like fruit than many a white burgundy of the

small-mortgage variety. I enjoy it as an aperitif, but grilled fish
is fine with it.

Sogrape Bairrada Reserva 1991   12   £D
Wood, wood, wood. You could built a tree house from the
wood in this wine.

ROMANIAN WINE – *red*

Pinot Noir 1988   16   £B
I was utterly bowled over by one sip of this wine. It has lovely
raspberry-tinged, woody fruit, husky, vegetal and mature, and
is of a quality which a rogue restaurateur could pass off as
forty-five quid burgundy.

Special Reserve Cabernet Sauvignon 1985   15   £B
Big, bright, fruity marvel for the money. Blackcurrant and
plums, vigorous, mouth-filling.

Special Reserve Merlot 1990   13   £B
Delicious lightly chilled.

SLOVENIAN WINE – *white*

Laski Rizling (Safeway)   10   £C

SOUTH AFRICAN WINE – *red*

De Helderbertg Cabernet Sauvignon, 1991	13	£C

Kanonkop Kadette 1991   15   £D
Sounds like the republic's first home-produced motor car instead of a vehicle for a load of tasty, fresh-faced fruit. A soft, aromatic wine, tinged by a suede-like dryness, which is just superb with roast meats.

Kanonkop Pinotage 1989   13   £E

Kleindal Pinotage 1992   15   £B
Great food wine and a brilliant bargain. Delicious, whizzbang firecracker fruit, dry, and a nutty finish.

SOUTH AFRICAN WINE – *white*

Bateleur Chardonnay 1992   14   £E
This is so elegant and delicious it's a special treat wine – there's nothing everyday about it.

Culemhof Colombard 1992   12   £B

Landskroom Pinot Blanc 1992   13   £D
Some elegant, delicious touches here.

Sauvignon Blanc, Vredendal 1991   12   £B

Swartland Stern 1992   14   £B
Delicious aperitif.

SPANISH WINE – *red*

Cariñena 1987 (Safeway)	13	£B

Don Darias 14 £B
You know how sometimes you meet an upfront fruity person whose ribald sense of humour almost makes you blush but you can't help yourself falling completely under his or her spell? So it is with this wine.

Raimat Merlot 1988 13 £D

Raimat Tempranillo 1988 15 £D
A marvellously ripe, oaky, blackcurranty wine for spicy Spanish food.

Rioja Crianza 1989 (Safeway) 13 £C

Valdepeñas 1987 13 £B

Valencia 1990 (Safeway) 10 £B

SPANISH WINE – *white and rosé*

La Mancha 1992 (Safeway) 13 £B
Excellent value party wine.

Penedès 1991 (Safeway) 12 £B

Rioja Rosé 1991 (Safeway) 13 £B

Valencia, Aged in Oak 1990 11 £B

Viña Ardanza, Rioja Reserva 1985 13 £E

Vino de Valencia Dry (Safeway) 14 £A

USA WINE – *red*

Fetzer Zinfandel 1990   16   £C
What an absolute devilish bottle of zin. Smells invitingly like
black cherry jam kept in an old leather purse and then delivers
lashing of full yet vigorous fruit. Huskily mature yet crazily
and zestfully youthful. Great stuff.

Ridge Paso Robles Zinfandel 1989   16   £E
Great fat clodfuls of earthy plums, cherries and goodness
knows what else pulse through this wine and it has gutsy
acidity to smooth the whole thing out so it offers the mellow
satisfaction of music played on a cello.

USA WINE – *white*

Californian White (Safeway)   12   £A
Not as keen on this wine as I once was. It's non-vintage, but
the wine changes from batch to batch and current delivery
doesn't excite me as much as previous ones. But it's straightforward, drinkable, and well-priced for all that.

Hawk Crest Chardonnay 1991   13   £D

Hidden Cellars Chardonnay 1991   13   £E
Agreeable touches of sticky apple and pineapple in the finish.
An organic wine.

WELSH WINE – *white*

Cariad Gwin da o Gymru 1990   12   £D
Balanced and reasonably dry with not unattractive soft fruit.
Certainly the greatest Welsh wine ever to pass my lips.

SPARKLING WINE/CHAMPAGNE

Albert Etienne Brut 1988 (Safeway)	12	£G
Albert Etienne Rosé (Safeway)	12	£F
Albert Etienne (Safeway)	13	£F
Angas Brut Rosé, Australia	15	£D
BB Club Brut, Hungary	15	£C

Under £4 for a sparkling wine? Okay, so it isn't hugely elegant
but I rate this bubbly for its attractive peachy fruit and vivacity.
I must admit I feel somewhat responsible for its presence on
Safeway shelves for I was at the winery in Hungry when the
winemaker said, during a tasting, 'Oh yes, we've also got a
sparkling wine. But I don't think you'll like it.' My enthusiasm
for this wine at this price was quite evident from one sip. I've
heard it described as rubbish by one wine writer, who has a
single cornflake for a brain, and I've listened to it being
equally slandered by a competitive supermarket wine buyer –
but he's merely jealous because he failed to spot the wine's
potential when he tasted it and never twigged how reasonably
it could be priced. Oh yes, the name's naff and the label's
even naffer. All adds to its charms, I say.

Billecart-Salmon Champagne 13 £G

Blancs de Blancs Brut, Les Dryades, France 15 £C
An utterly beguilingly lemony sparkler of huge charm and drinkability for just over a fiver and good enough for anyone's wedding.

Blanquette de Limoux, Bernard Delmas 13 £D
An organic sparkler full of delicious peachy/nutty fruit.

Bolero 13 £B
This is a 5.5% sweet fruit wine from Austria, made from peaches and apricots, which is hugely amusing: one bottle I opened kept its bubbles for 72 hours and still frothed at me for a little time after. Makes an excellent basis for a stiffer cocktail or, by itself, is good for uncritical teenagers and toothless old crones who nevertheless lay claim to possessing a sweet tooth.

Bollinger Special Cuvée Brut 12 £H
Over twenty quid: is it worth it? I wish I could provide a wholehearted yes, in spite of Bollinger's very particular dry charms.

Cava (Safeway) (magnum) 13 £F
Buy it for the style and the big fat bottle.

Chardonnay Spumante (Safeway) 13 £D
Very pleasant champagne substitute.

Chartogne-Taillet Champagne Brut 13 £G

**Crémant de Bourgogne Blanc de Blancs
(Safeway)** 13 £D

Cuvée Napa, USA 14 £E
Compares to a classic brut champagne in style.

Freixenet Cordon Negro Brut Cava   13   £D

**Le Grand Pavillon de Boschendale, Cuvée Brut
Blanc de Blancs, South Africa**   16   £D
Refreshing, stylish, and tastes like a grand marque champagne
at three times the price. Brilliant sparkler to mystify your wine
buff acquaintances.

Lindauer Brut, New Zealand   13   £D

Lionel Derens champagne   15   £E
A dry fruity champagne, without the intimidating acidity of
the classic brut examples. This is a very satisfying tipple and at
under £9 a good price.

Seppelt Premier Cuvée Brut Australia   15   £D
Under-six-quid marvel – elegant, stylish and it looks a treat
on the table as well as in the glass.

Sparkling Blackcurrant   15   £B
This is pure unadulterated blackcurrant in smell and taste.
This is not surprising, since no grape gets a look in, just
blackcurrants. It is great fun and a hilarious addition to a party
or to a Christmas lunch – even at 5.5% alcohol.

Sainsbury's

For years, this store was the Liverpool F.C. of supermarket wine buying. It won everything there was to win, scored more goals, played to the biggest crowds. It even had a wine manager in the Bill Shankly mould but then, as is the Sainsbury way and arguably the unique strength of the store, he had to move on after his tour of duty to oversee fruit and vegetable buying and a new manager took over with a different attitude. (Which illustrates, incidentally, why supermarket wine buyers, notwithstanding their obviously huge buying power, are such strong negotiators. They are *buyers* first and foremost and only secondarily are they *wine* buyers. This not only means a complete lack of pretension, it also results in an utter dedication to getting the right quality product at the right price underpinned by an absolute grasp of the vital importance of price points to customers.) The new man saw things differently; he had his own game plan. He was going to encourage his team of buyers to do things its own way, allowing these various individuals – each with a portfolio of countries to call his or her own – to experiment a bit more and even make a few mistakes. He was going to allow them, young, enthusiastic and still swotting for their Master of Wine exams, to stick out their necks and their noses and scour the whole world for newer and better bargains. He was even going to let them persuade winemakers from one continent to fly across the world and make wine in another continent. He was going to allow them to make positive suggestions to winemakers – and winemakers are not always a suggestible or tractable lot. The competition was getting better, tougher, more purposeful and more ruthlessly competitive, every year – how could the store

stand still? Building on the strength of its wine-buying reputation and prowess, this new-look Sainsbury's wine-buying
department has come up with a whole range of interesting
new wines from every corner of the globe. And many of the
best of them are the direct result of this restless globe-
trotting, and unflinching nose-stick-outing, that these young
buyers have been encouraged to embark on as never before.
And if one word sums up these new Sainsbury wines it is fruit
– fruit of all flavours and all textures.

Indeed, Sainsbury's buyers' enthusiasm and commitment
knows no bounds, as I discovered at great risk to my own
health and well-being when I accompanied two of them on a
two-day trip to Italy. Within the space of 48 hours I was
whisked by Alitalia from Heathrow to Milan, driven at break-
neck speed to Novara, 50km west, where I had dinner at
half-past one in the morning, to be woken early next day, so
early indeed that the Piemontese sparrows were actually
yawning as we sped past, to drive off and taste the co-op wines
for breakfast, then to be driven 100km over to Barolo for
elevenses, then hair-pinned all the way to Asti for more red
wines and a Lynford-Christie-quick lunch of chunks of par-
mesan before being driven to Genoa airport from where a
plane took us to Naples, thence to be driven through the night
to Basilicata, which only the day before had been cut off by
aggressively unseasonable eight-foot drifts of snow, to stay in
one of the few hotels in this neglected southern province, only
to enjoy another dawn start so as to arrive at the local co-op
and to enjoy their wines for breakfast. On to Lecce on the
Adriatic coast, a journey of several hundred kilometres, for a
late lunch of a sandwich and a glass of wine, after which we
drove to Brindisi, flew to Milan, then took another plane to
Heathrow where I fled gratefully into the secure and plodding
clutches of the London underground. 'Relaxing trip?' said my

wife as I came through the door and collapsed into her arms.

High-speed wine buyers, in a world of tighter profit margins and intense competition, need to go where the bargains are and where quality either exists or can be encouraged to exist. Italy is a case in point: unlike other European wine-producing countries, it has a currency which is weak against the pound and so a bargain can more easily be struck. Of the four Sainsbury wines I tasted on that trip, all are good (one is exceptional), all are terrific value, and if the prices can be maintained they will, I am sure, become favourites amongst Sainsbury's red wine customers. You'll find all the wines in this book and they are Spanna, Basilicata red and white, and Copertino Riserva.

ARGENTINIAN WINE – *red*

Cavas de Weinert, Mendoza, 1985   14   £D
Delightful – dry, dusky, hearty, with a heart of gentle chocolate.

Malbec/Cabernet (Sainsbury's)   12   £B
Delicious cherryade.

Trapiche Cabernet Sauvignon 1987   13   £C

Trapiche Oak Cask Cabernet Sauvignon 1986   14   £C
Dry, very dry – very mature and tasty. Great big flavour and style.

ARGENTINIAN WINE – *white*

Torrontes 1993 (Sainsbury's) 14 £B

Delicious aroma, taste and overall balance. Lots of fruit, good length. Excellent value. Excellent fish wine.

Trapiche Oak Cask Chardonnay 1992 15 £C

Wood-lovers' wine. Quite delicious. Very stylish, very sophisticated.

AUSTRALIAN WINE – *red*

Hardys Stamp Series Shiraz/Cabernet Sauvignon 1991 13 £C

Lindemans Pyrus 1988 15 £E

Lovely subtle eucalyptus touches to the fruit – incredibly unctuous fruit, velvet, soft, yielding.

Nottage Hill Cabernet Sauvignon 1991 15 £C

Simply and utterly delicious – great style – lovely soft berries, tarry and rich.

Orlando St Hugo Cabernet Sauvignon 1989 17 £E

As aromatically compelling as new leather in a brand new limousine. Soft, effortlessly contrived, velvet and silken fruit. Plums, cherries, figs and cream. Sheer poison – to many a French wine-grower.

Penfolds Bin 389 Cabernet/Shiraz 1989 15 £D

Matured in ex-Grange Hermitage casks (which once contained what is widely considered to be Australia's greatest red wine – though the benefits of this are arguably no more enhancing than you or me slipping on Man. United's No. 10 shirt). Superb style, stretched fruit, very thought-provoking.

**Penfolds Koonunga Hill Shiraz/Cabernet
Sauvignon 1991**   13   £C

Rosemount Cabernet/Shiraz 1991   15   £D
Superb soft leathery fruit. Spicy (which is subtle). Very elegant. Polished performance all round.

St-Hallett Cabernet Merlot 1990   15   £D
Lovely wine of unusually seductive and softly whispering, yet confident hoity-toity fruit. Who said there's no such animal as an Australian aristocrat?

Shiraz/Cabernet (Sainsbury's)   15   £B
Rich and meaty, savoury and velvety – this is an outstanding roast fowl wine. Has gusto and guts. Sheer gustatory delight.

**South East Australia Cabernet Sauvignon
Bin 937, Wyndham Estate 1991**   14   £C
Plums and raisins. Dry, delicious.

**South East Australia Shiraz Bin 822, Wyndham
Estate 1991**   15   £C
Froths with flavoursome fruits, drily conceived but sweetly expressed.

AUSTRALIAN WINE – *white*

Australian Chardonnay, Riverina (Sainsbury's)   15   £C
Lush fruit, pineappley and melony, with lemony acidity. Great style for the money. An oaky, deliciously fruity wine which is

brilliant value under four quid. It has so much balance and style, it's difficult to think of any winemaker making tastier chardonnay for the money.

Berri Estates Wood-aged Chardonnay 1990   14   £D
What an old dog of a wine! The fruit just snarls at you and bristles with flavour. Wonderful with a herb-drenched roast chicken.

Chenin/Chardonnay (Sainsbury's)   15   £B
For style, value for money, enough fruit yet not over-the-top oakiness and tinned pineappliness, this wine takes the biscuit – especially one spread with fish pâté.

Hardy Collection Chardonnay 1990   15   £D
So rich it clogs the throat. Gorgeous soft fruit threaded through with citric flavour.

Hunter Valley Chardonnay, Denman Estate 1992 (Sainsbury's)   14   £C
A finely tuned exercise in plum and melon fruit with a subtle citric orange undertone. Luxury under a fiver.

Jacob's Creek Semillon/Chardonnay 1992   13   £C

Jacob's Creek Chardonnay 1992   15   £C
Oily and elongated – quite superb fruit. Hedonistic wine.

Koonunga Hill Chardonnay 1992   14   £C
Don't like its proximity to a fiver but do admire its proximity to an outstanding bottle of chardonnay – with mussels cooked the Thai way with lemon grass, this rich, rippling-with-fruit wine is a perfect fruit relish accompaniment.

Krondorf Show Reserve Chardonnay 1991   14   £E
My vocabulary is becoming stretched trying to pin down

effably yet another antipodean taste-bud titillation comprised of chardonnay grapes.

Lindemans Bin 65 Chardonnay 1992   15   £C
Delicious *divertissement* for lovers of rich wines. Great style. Immensely palatable, pacy fruit.

Mitchelton Marsanne 1990   14   £D
Fleshy, well-developed, stylish and almost impetuously fruity.

Mitchelton Semillon 1988   14   £D
Very rich and offering enough fruit to wallow in.

Moondah Brook Estate Chenin Blanc 1992   15   £C
Utterly captivating wine. Fabulous steel-jacketed melon fruit.

Rosemount Estate Chardonnay/Semillon 1992   14   £C
Lovely, fresh-faced wine for fish (grilled or roasted).

Sandalford Verdelho, Margaret River   15   £D
Great fruit, great acid – what a captivatingly well-balanced mouthful! Brilliant wine.

Tasmanian Wine Company Chardonnay 1991   14   £E
A superb aperitif. You could eat a horse after downing a glass of this wine.

Tyrrells Old Winery Chardonnay 1992   15   £D
The usual fruit medley, but with a really exciting lime finish.

AUSTRIAN WINE – *white*

Bouvier Trockenbeerenauslese 1989 (half)   13   £D
A little treat for the solo diner with a bunch of black grapes and a chunk of blue cheese.

BULGARIAN WINE – *red*

Bulgarian Cabernet Sauvignon (Sainsbury's)   14   £B
Excellent dry varietal style and fruit. Brilliant value. Good wine
for food, particularly roast meat.

Bulgarian Merlot (Sainsbury's)   13   £B
Good style. Good, rich, meaty fruit. Good value.

**Country Wine Russe Cabernet Sauvignon/
Cinsault (Sainsbury's)**   13   £B

**Country Wine Suhindol Merlot/Gamza
(Sainsbury's)**   12   £B

Lovico Suhindol Cabernet Sauvignon Reserve   13   £B
Excellent dry style.

Lovico Suhindol Merlot Reserve   14   £B
Delicious soft plummy wine with a faint hint of liquorice and
mint.

Stambolovo Merlot Special Reserve 1986   12   £D

BULGARIAN WINE – *white*

**Bulgarian Country Wine Muskat and Ugni
Blanc (Sainsbury's)**   13   £B
Very attractive, powder-compact soft fruit undercut by a
tingling freshness. Good value.

**Bulgarian Country Wine Riesling and
Dimiat (Sainsbury's)**   12   £B
At this price, this has great attractions – as does the wine's fruit.

Khan Krum Chardonnay Reserve 1990   13   £B
Excellent value chardonnay of some varietal strength.

Welsch-Riesling (Sainsbury's)   13   £E

CHILEAN WINE – *red*

Caliterra Cabernet Sauvignon 1990   13   £C

CHILEAN WINE – *white*

Caliterra Sauvignon Blanc 1992   15   £C
A nervous, quiet but attractively elegant wine, the fruitiness of
which disappears with rich dishes so respect its rectitude and
subtle lemon and melon fruit by drinking it alone or with light
quiches and salads. Good with grilled squid rings with lemon
and no sauce.

Chilean Sauvignon Blanc 1992   13   £B

Santa Rita Chardonnay 1990   13   £D

Santa Rita Medalla Real Chardonnay 1991   15   £D
Oily rich fruit. Much style, soft and unguent. Great with
smoked trout, mackerel, eel.

CHINESE WINE – *white*

Tsingtao Chardonnay 1988   11   £C

ENGLISH WINE – *white*

Denbies Estate English Table Wine 1991   13 £C
Delicious, off-dry melony wine. Aromatic, stylish and very fruity.

Hastings, Carr Taylor   14 £C
One of my favourite English wines for it has a lot of decent fruit and a keen sense of balance.

Lamberhurst   14 £C
One of the better English wines which prompts the thought that if they were all this tasty, and under £3, muscadet makers would have to think of turning to apple growing to make a living.

Three Choirs Seyval Reichensteiner   12 £C
Not the 14 point dry version but a medium dry.

FRENCH WINE – *red*

A Year in Provence 1991   10 £C
Many a stuck-up pseud in the travel, food and wine writing fraternity loathes the success of the superb little soufflé of a book this wine is named after. Alas, this wine was released in March to coincide with the screening of the worst BBC-TV serial of the past decade – a catalogue of disaster which bore little relation to the book. Peter Mayle may take consolation for this TV flop from this bottle – or he may not.

Anjou Rouge (Sainsbury's)   10 £B

Beaujolais (Sainsbury's)   11 £C

Beaujolais-Villages, Les Roches Grillées 1992   14 £C
One of the more respectably decent Bs on sale.

Bergerac Rouge (Sainsbury's)   12 £B

**Bergerie de l'Arbous, Coteaux du
Languedoc 1990**   13 £C

Bourgueil 1992   14 £C
Wild, delicious raspberry fruit. Will improve over the next
year.

**Cabernet Sauvignon, Vin de Pays d'Oc
(3 litres)**   12 £F

Cahors (Sainsbury's)   14 £B
Bargain price for a rich dark wine which is brilliant with
grilled food. Chewy like coal, but a lot, lot softer to swallow.

**Chais Baumière Cabernet Sauvignon, Vin de
Pays d'Oc 1991**   14 £C
Soft, stylish, delicious.

Chais Baumière Merlot 1990   15 £C
This merlot is from an Australian-owned and managed vineyard (Hardys) in the Languedoc. It is dry and savoury in the
way merlots can be and the fruit has echoes of wood, spice
and tobacco, which all make it an excellent companion to
herby roasts and stews. Interestingly, I have drunk this wine
six miles up in the sky, courtesy of British Airways, but I
must say I prefer the wine at ground level.

Château Barreyres, Haut-Médoc 1988   14 £D
The bitter fruit is well harnessed by the aroma. A very good
value bottle for the seriousness of the wine.

Château Camarsac 1989, Sainsbury's Bordeaux 14 £C
A delightfully approachable claret of soft, stylish fruit.

Château Cantemerle Haut-Médoc 1987 12 £G

Château Crillon, Côtes du Ventoux 1990 12 £C

Château d'Aigueville, Côtes du Rhône 1990 13 £C
Reliable as ever. Very attractive fruit and style.

Château de Bousquet, Côtes de Bourg 1990 15 £D
This has an intriguing chocolate richness (plus a subtle liquorice tone). Splendid opportunity to buy a cheap claret which will age well and soften even further.

Château de Gourgazaud, Minervois 1990 15 £B
Lovely sweet fruit finish to the overall dry style.

Château de Turegand Pecharment Bergerac 1990 14 £D
An extremely classy roast lamb wine. Certainly justifies fine china and candles.

Château La Vieille Cure, Fronsac 1989 14 £E
Brilliant, but keep for two or three years more and it'll be even smoother and richer.

Château Maucaillou, Moulis 1989 13 £F

Château Moulin du Breuil, Haut-Médoc 1989 15 £E
Lovely brambly fruit and teeth-clenching tannic softness. Will get even fancier over the next two to three years.

Château Rozier, St-Emilion Grand Cru 1989 12 £E

Château Salvanhiac, St-Chinian 1992 12 £B

Châteauneuf-du-Pape, Les Galets Blancs 1991 12 £D
In a lighter and less bloody vein than most Châteauneufs.

Chinon, Domaine du Colombier 1991   13   £D
This will soften over 1994 to become the 15-pointer previous
vintages have been.

Claret Bordeaux Supérieur (Sainsbury's)   13   £B

Côtes Rôtie, Delas 1987   11   £F

**Côtes du Frontonnais, Château Bellevue la
Forêt 1991**   14   £C
Lovely style – chewy and dry yet soft and fruity. Jam with a
crust.

Côtes du Luberon (Sainsbury's)   11   £B

Côtes du Rhône Villages, Beaumes de Venise   13   £C

Côtes du Rhône (Sainsbury's)   14   £B
Can there be a softer, more attractively earthy CdR on sale for
the money?

Crozes-Hermitage   13   £C
Bit of an acquired taste this one (also a touch pricey). Like
chewing light bulbs and rich plums. I don't dislike this sort of
mouthful. I enjoyed this wine with herb-drenched, chargrilled
lamb chops.

Domaine du Révérend, Corbières 1989   14   £C
Tar and rosewater entwined with the soft berried fruit.

Fiefs de Lagrange, St-Julien 1987   15   £E
Grassy on the nose then the richness and complexity wallops
the palate and you think, 'This is good old-style claret without
tannic unfriendliness'. A very companionable wine with fine
food: elegant, distinguished in a slightly raffish sense and very
warmly fruity.

Fitou, Les Guèches 1990   13   £B

Fleurie, La Madone, 1991   12   £D

Fortant Collection Cabernet Sauvignon, Vin de Pays d'Oc 1990   13   £D
Delicious.

Gigondas Tour du Queyron 1990   15   £E
Expensive but expansive. Big, hearty, huge, smoky fruit. Concentrated soft centre. Lovely wine.

Graves Selection Sainsbury's, Louis Vialard   13   £C
Good soft fruit.

Hauts Côtes de Nuits, Les Dames Huguettes 1990   12   £E

Madiran, Château de Crouseilles 1988   14   £D
Stylish dry beauty with lots of soft berried fruit.

Mondot, St-Emilion 1989   13   £E

Moulin à Vent, Cave Kuhnel 1990   11   £D

Red Burgundy Pinot Noir (Sainsbury's)   12   £C
Interesting that this wine should so boldly state its grape when, as is not exactly a French state secret, red Burgundy is exclusively 100 per cent pinot noir and has been for several centuries (they got rid of the gamay to Beaujolais in 1393). Could it be that the success of pinots from other countries, and labelled as such, has made someone somewhere conscious that Burgundy needs to compete with this and varietally label its wine to match? Tut, tut.

Réserve de la Comtesse, Pauliac 1988   11   £F
Scores a point more than last year so it must be improving. But will it reach 20 points by 2002? I wouldn't put my money on it.

Vin de Pays de la Cité de Carcassonne
Merlot 1992 (Sainsbury's)   12   £B

FRENCH WINES – *white and rosé*

Alsace Gewürztraminer (Sainsbury's)   13   £C

Alsace Pinot Blanc (Sainsbury's)   13   £C

Bergerac Blanc (Sainsbury's)   13   £B

Blanc de Blancs (Sainsbury's)   14   £B
Modern, star-bright, fresh and pear-and-melon-drop fruity.
A delightful little wine for fish parties. Bargain.

Bordeaux Sauvignon (Sainsbury's)   12   £B

Chablis 1992, Madeleine Mathieu   13   £D
Great stuff.

Chais Baumière Chardonnay, Vin de Pays
d'Oc 1991   15   £C
Lovely oily fruit on the tongue and a subtle lemony finish in
the throat. An excellent bottle.

Chais Baumière Sauvignon Blanc, Vin de Pays d'Oc
1992   15   £C
Excellent balance, fruit and acid in nice harmony. Classy and
stylish. Great aperitif or with fish and shellfish.

Chardonnay, Vin de Pays d'Oc Ryman 1992   13   £C
Good style.

Château de Davenay, Montagny Premier
Cru 1990   12   £D

Château Mayne des Carmes, Sauternes 1989   15   £G
Very fine, very fine indeed. Like an angel pissing on your
tongue.

Château Rocheblanche, Bordeaux Blanc 1992   13   £B
Surprising level of attractive fruit for a wine from this area at
this price.

Châteauneuf-du-Pape André Brunel 1992   14   £E
If you like wine this soft, seductive and purring like a pussy
cat, your money's well spent.

Clos l'Abeilly, Sauternes 1990 (half)   13   £C

Clos St-Georges, Graves Supérieures 1990   15   £E
Try this as an aperitif. It's wonderful even though it's honeyed
and toffeed.

Corbières Blanc (Sainsbury's)   12   £B

Costières de Nîmes 1992 (Sainsbury's)   13   £B
Very attractive.

Coteaux du Languedoc (Sainsbury's)   14   £B
A delicious, nutty, fruity, clean-finishing white wine at a
bargain price.

**Côtes de Provence, Les Vignerols 1992
(Sainsbury's)**   12   £C
Some attractive fruit here.

Côtes de Duras (Sainsbury's)   13   £B

Côtes du Rhône, La Meynarde 1992   12   £C

**Domaine de Grandchamp Sauvignon Blanc,
Bergerac 1992**   15   £D
Delightful grass, lemon zest and plum fruit. A touch of New

Zealand freshness to southern French flavours. Made in the château owned by Hugh Ryman's dad in the Dordogne.

Domaine de la Tuilerie Rosé 1991   13   £C

Domaine des Blancs, Côtes du Luberon Rosé 1991   14   £B
An admirable example of an otherwise deservedly despised genre. Excellent with smoked fish.

Duc Dupeyron, Bordeaux 1990   15   £D
A distinguished combination of glossy fruit and fine-grained wood.

Fortant Collection Chardonnay, Vin de Pays d'Oc 1991   14   £D
Very classy, very very classy. Beautifully developed fruit.

Mâcon Blanc Villages, Domaine les Chenevières 1991 (half)   13   £C
A chewy treat for the white burgundy lover on his or her tod.

Mâcon Blanc Villages, Domaine les Chenevières 1992   13   £C
Very good style. A true minor burgundy at a good price.

Mâcon Chardonnay 1991, Domaines les Ecuyers   13   £D

Menetou Salon 1992, Domaine Henri Pelle   14   £D
Sancerre ringer. Good old-fashioned likeness, too.

Mersault Blagny, Premier Cru, Gérard Thomas 1990   14   £G
This is quite, quite gorgeous, in a lighter style than typical: woody fruit, elegantly turned. Lovely.

Mouton Cadet 1991 10 £C
Hold your breath and listen: 'Beautiful straw colour with good
highlights. The generous nose is forward and full, with notes
of grilled almonds. On the palate the wine is round and well
evolved, combining body and fruit. Well structured, with great
aromatic complexity. Very good length, offering richness,
finesse and balance.' So say the Rothschilds about this, their
wine. All I can say is they should have added a rider about this
drinkable but crazily overpriced wine going extremely well
with fish, particularly codswallop.

Muscadet de Sèvre-et-Maine (Sainsbury's) 13 £B
A lot of fruit for a muscadet.

Muscadet de Sèvre-et-Maine Sur Lie,
Château de la Dimerie 1992 13 £C
Attractive fruity specimen.

Muscadet de Sèvre-et-Maine Sur Lie,
Premierè Jean Drouillard, 1990 13 £D

Muscadet, Domaine du Bois Bruley 1990 11 £C

Muscat de Saint-Jean de Minervois (half) 14 £B
Sweet satin.

Pouilly-Fuissé, Domaine Henri Carrette 1990 12 £E

Pouilly-Fuissé, Laboure Roi 1991 12 £D

Pouilly-Fumé le Bouchaud, Fouassier 1992 13 £E

Premières Côtes de Bordeaux 11 £C

Puligny Montrachet, Domaine Gérard Chavy
1991 10 £F

Sancerre Les Beaux Regards 1992   14   £E
Still one of the best supermarket sancerres on sale.

**Saumur Blanc, Domaine des Hauts de Sanziers
1991**   12   £D
Lip-puckering curiosity of interest to live shellfish eaters.

Tokay Pinot Gris, Cave de Ribeauville 1989   16   £E
Brilliant apricot aroma. Captivating fruit of great concentration of flavour and complexity and firmness of finish. A superb
bottle of wine.

Touraine Sauvignon Blanc (Sainsbury's)   13   £B
Attractive fruit, lemon-edged.

Vin de Pays d'Oc Chardonnay (3 litres)   12   £G

Vin de Pays d'Oc (Sainsbury's)   13   £B
Admirable richness of fruit. Good price.

**Vin de Pays d'Oc Sauvignon Blanc, Domaine
St-Marc 1992**   14   £C
Very attractive concentration of fruit. New World meets Old.

Vin de Pays d'Oc Sur Lie   13   £B

**Vin de Pays de Gascogne, Domaine Bordes
1992**   14   £B
Delicious, delicious, delicious! Alive with electric fruit!!

**Vin de Pays des Côtes de Gascogne
(Sainsbury's)**   14   £B
One of the most attractive white Gascons on sale: lush fruit
and flint-edged. Lovely style for the money.

Vin de Pays du Gers (Sainsbury's)   14   £B
A lovely refreshing mouthful. Terrific price for this quality of
fruit and structure.

**Viognier, Vin de Pays des Coteaux de l'Ardéche,
1992, Cévennes Ardéchoise**   14   £C
Delightful soft fruit, plums and ogen melon and peach.
Lovely.

Vouvray Demi-Sec (Sainsbury's)   12   £C
Delicious aperitif if you can take the toffee sweetness.

White Burgundy Chardonnay (Sainsbury's)   13   £D

GERMAN WINE – *white*

**Auslese Bereich Mittelhaardt 1990
(Sainsbury's)**   15   £C
This is such a beautifully rich, fragrant, fruity wine (ripe pears
and lychees), cut through with the unique acidic gorgeousness
of the riesling grape, that with ham dishes, or with a complex
creation like coronation chicken, it adds both a dimension of
its own and cutting relief from the smoky spiciness of the
food. I should add that I also enjoy this wine by itself at the
end of a workday.

Baden Dry (Sainsbury's)   14   £B
Subtly spicy and fruity and excellent value.

Baden Pinot Blanc Dry 1989   13   £C

Dornfelder Trocken 1991   12   £C

**Kabinett Sainsbury's, Dalsheimer Burg
Rodenstein 1991**   13   £B
A terrific aperitif.

Morio Muskat (Sainsbury's)   12   £B

Niersteiner Gutes Domtal (Sainsbury's)   12   £A

**Spätlese Mosel-Saar-Ruwer, Bernkasteler
Kurfurstlay 1991 (Sainsbury's)**   12   £C

Trocken Rheinhessen (Sainsbury's)   11   £B

GREEK WINE – *white*

Retsina   13   £B
Resinated and fruity, but also clean to finish, and at under £3
I find this wine both a bargain and excellent with grilled fish as
well as, of course, Greek starters.

HUNGARIAN WINE – *red*

**Hungarian Cabernet Sauvignon, Balaton Boglar
1986**   14   £D
Aromatically indistinguishable, by a 6½-year-old child given
a glass of each, from Ribena. This wine is all blackcurrant.
Where did the tannin and acid go? Wallow and enjoy (with any
roast meats). You could spread it on toast at breakfast, it's so
jammy.

Merlot (Sainsbury's)   14   £B

HUNGARIAN WINE – *white and rosé*

Chapel Hill Chardonnay, Balaton Boglar 1992   13   £B
Nice weight of fruit, even nicer lack of weight of price.

**Chapel Hill Sauvignon Blanc Balaton Boglar
1992   13   £B**
Remarkable price for a decently rich wine.

Country White Wine (Sainsbury's)   14   £B
Can't argue with this level of old world fruit and new world
acidity. Fantastic value.

Gyöngyös Estate Chardonnay 1992   14   £B
Rich, well-rounded. Attractive fruit, attractive price. Amazing
what you can get out of a coal town in the middle of Hungary
when you really try.

Gyöngyös Estate Country Wine   13   £B
Komaron is the name of the grape but it's merely a cover for
semillon (an unofficial variety here). The result of this decep-
tion is a decently rich fruity wine at a decent price.

Gyöngyös Estate Sauvignon Blanc, Ryman 1992 14   £B
Good rich fruit, well-structured and finished. Delicious
lemony finish. Excellent value. Lively and very attractive.

Hungarian Pinot Blanc (Sainsbury's)   15   £B
At this price, this wine is a superbly drinkable bargain. It's
fruity and clean and so saddled with thoroughbred elegance
and poise that it overshadows many a wine asking three times
the price (like some Loire sauvignons), as would an Arab
stallion a carthorse.

Nagyrede Cabernet Sauvignon Rosé 1992   15   £B
Raspberries and peardrops were this rosé's abiding memories,
from when I first tasted it in late January in the winery itself,
situated a few hours' car ride from Budapest, but at a more
recent slurp-in the wine offered up a lovely aroma of the
setting sun on a Provençal peach orchard after a hot day's
baking. This is a delicious oxymoronic rosé: you can take it
seriously lightly. It has a perfect weight of alcohol (11.5%),
great balance as it pirouettes on the tongue and an excellent
price.

ITALIAN WINE – *red*

Barbaresco 1987   13   £E
Hairy beast. Very dry.

Bardolino Classico (Sainsbury's)   13   £B
Cherries and white chocolate.

Basilicata   14   £B
Has a gentle plum fruitiness, with a distinctive mineral edge
the area's volcanic soil bestows on its grapes, and this makes it
a terrific glugging wine or with pastas.

**Castello di San Polo in Rosso, Chianti
Classico 1988**   15   £D
Rich velvet soaked in blackberries with a lush cherry acid
balance. Oleaginous, sinuous, wickedly fruity, it is simply one
of the loveliest chiantis on sale. A smash hit with grilled or
roasted herby food.

Chianti (Sainsbury's)   14   £B

Chianti Classico, Barone Ricasoli 1989
(Sainsbury's)   16   £C
Perfectly mature, soft with that touch of Tuscan terracotta
(baked earth) quality to the fruit. Utterly delicious with grilled
vegetables on which garlic and green and pungently peppery
Tuscan virgin olive oil has been sprinkled. But take the veg
away and you've still got one hell of a classy bottle.

Copertino Riserva 1989   15   £C
This wine from Lecce on the Adriatic is all local grape
varieties, mostly negro amaro, and it is a deep sturdy mature
red, dry, husky, and richly fruity with undertones of coffee
and tobacco (all smoothed out as a result of its oak ageing). It
is an old leather armchair of a wine in some respects and for
under £4 it is a seriously toothsome bargain.

Nivola, Lambrusco Montovano Secco   10   £B
Secco? Secco? Maybe they think secco means saccharine.
Certainly this wine has sweetness added to take it away from
the true, lip-puckering, adenoid-crushing whiplash-clean
home-grown Lambrusco style (see Safeway for the real
thing).

San Lorenzo Rosso Conero Umani Ronchi 1988 14   £C
Smooth, voluptuous, and bursting with enterprising fruit, it's
like being whacked in the kisser with soft new leather and
dark cherries when you touch this wine. Only pity is it's over a
fiver.

Sicilian Red (Sainsbury's)   14   £B
Brilliant pasta-eaters' bargain. Soft, touch of sunny earth –
good finish. Excellent stuff for the money.

Spanna del Piemonte   14 £B

This has youth on its side. It's a nebbiolo wine, the grape
variety which makes Barolo, but there's not an echo of that
classic wine's liquorice-rich fruit in this raspberry and cherry-
ish specimen, which is a pleasant, relaxing hammock of a
wine, even better left to breathe for a couple of hours, and
another outright bargain at £2.69. It rates 14 points. I truly
wonder if I shouldn't rate it higher. But considering what I
went through to taste this wine (please refer to Introduction),
it's a miracle I'm still on drinking terms with it.

Valpolicella Classico, Negarine 1990
(Sainsbury's)   16 £B

I mistakenly gave this wine a rating of 116 after I drank it –
and I wonder if it wasn't wishful thinking but really the way I
actually feel about this staggeringly toothsome savoury-edged
cherry/raspberry/plum wine which is one of the nattiest wines
around for the money.

Valpolicella Classico, Negarine 1991
(Sainsbury's)   13 £B

13 points at time of tasting but the '89 and '90 are terrific
15/16 pointers and I see no reason to disbelieve this '91 won't
be up here by Xmas '93 and beyond.

Valpolicella Classico (Sainsbury's)   12 £B

Vino Nobile di Montepulciano, Fattoria di
Casale 1988   13 £D

Winemaker's Choice, Vino da Tavola Rosso   11 £B

ITALIAN WINE – *white*

Avignonesi Bianco Sauvignon-Chardonnay 1991	12	£D

Basilicata 14 £B
This white has a delicious mineral bite to it, a good level of fruit, and not only is it an excellent aperitif but a superb wine for fresh oysters and other such *fruits de mer*.

Bianco di Custoza 1992 14 £B
Full fruit, lemon-edged. Delicious wine.

Chardonnay Alto Adige 1991 (Sainsbury's) 14 £C

Chardonnay delle Tre Venezie (Sainsbury's) 15 £C
Excellent style, excellent value. Lovely balanced fruit, freshness and finish.

Cortese Alto Monferrato (Sainsbury's) 13 £B
Excellent with fish and salad starters.

Garganega Sauvignon 1991 (Sainsbury's) 13 £C

Gavi, Bersano 1991 13 £C

Graffitti, Est! Est!! Est!!! Bigi 1992 14 £C
OK, the label does look like it's been designed by the guy who creates Barbie doll cosmetics but it's an accurate portrayal of the curiously powder-compact fruit, soft and feathery, within the bottle. I love its gulpability and though it has a tough time finding a partner to waltz with on the plate, it's a terrific aperitif. Every time I write about this wine and say what a daft name it has I get at least six letters from failed Mastermind contestants proudly explaining to me the utterly banal reasons for the name. Save yourself the postage and use your lips to

get stuck into the wine instead is my advice, for this is easily
the most delicious bottle of this daftly named, daftly labelled,
daftly fruity wine I've ever drunk.

Lugana San Benedetto Zenato 1992   14   £C
Classy, stylish – quite superb.

Pinot Grigio del Veneto (Sainsbury's)   14   £B
A new blend and a much better wine than previous bottles.
Lots of good rich fruit.

Sicilian White (Sainsbury's)   14   £B
Not a lean mean Sicilian but a full-flavoured, even meaty,
wine yet clean and fresh to finish. Great value.

Soave Classico Costalunga Pasqua 1992   13   £C
Delicious, fruity soave which goes some way to restoring the
reputation of this often bland dull wine.

Tocai del Veneto (3 litres)   11   £F

Trebbiano di Romagna (Sainsbury's) (1.5 litres) 13   £C

Verduzzo del Piave (Sainsbury's)   13   £B

Vernaccia di San Gimignano, San Quirico 1991 13   £C

Winemaker's Choice   12   £B

LEBANESE WINE – *red*

Château Musar 1986   16   £D
Inevitably, this ultimate stuffed-turkey wine has gone up in
price. From under a fiver when the first edition of this book
came out to now touching £7.50. But it's still a great wine and

even if a 50% price hike in so short a time is difficult to
follow, the wine is one of the easiest: rich, dark, almost cloying
spicy fruit, a touch exotic, a touch nervous, this is a remarkable wine by anyone's book.

NEW ZEALAND WINE – *red*

Cook's Cabernet Merlot 1990	13	£C
Montana Cabernet Sauvignon Marlborough 1991	13	£C

NEW ZEALAND WINE – *white*

Babich Irongate Chardonnay 1991   14   £F
There are some sauternes which smell less enticingly rich
than this dry wine which is the colour of freshly waxed young
oak parquet flooring. Oleaginous and rich and so grateful for
food it'll lie down and die with smoked salmon doused in
lemon juice and liberally sprinkled with black pepper.

Chenin Chardonnay (Sainsbury's)   13   £C

Delegats Fern Hills Sauvignon Blanc 1992   16   £C
One of the loveliest of the new-wave Kiwis, this one. Lots of
keen herbaceous fruit, subtly sherry-like in a most engaging
way, and a terrific finish of freshness, flavour and style. Great
value for such conspicuous classiness.

Matua Valley Sauvignon Blanc 1991   13   £D
Rather acquired concentrated grassy character.

Montana Church Road Chardonnay, Hawkes Bay 1992   16   £E
Knock-out. Buttery fruit, all enriched with a soft woodiness plus pineapple acidity. Delicious.

Montana Sauvignon Blanc, Marlborough 1992   13   £C
Delicious grass-edged fruit.

Nobilo Chardonnay, Poverty Bay 1992   14   £C
Peachy fruit, delicious and refreshing. Lovely wine.

Nobilo White Cloud 1992   13   £C
Firm, fresh finish to this very attractive wine.

Oyster Bay Chardonnay, Hawkes Bay 1992   15   £E
Sheer delight. What a glorious bottle for fried scallops! Heaven!

PORTUGUESE WINE – *red*

Alentejo 1989   15   £B
This Alentejo, so named from its area of growth (which is vying with certain parts of eastern Europe to be the hot spot to watch), is dry, dusty, yet has lots of richness and freshness, typically Portuguese in many respects yet also very 1990s, and with its chunky meaty fruit would be excellent with stews and roasts. A terrific little wine for well under £3.50.

Arruda (Sainsbury's)   14   £B
Burly fruit, yet balanced and dry. One of this book's long-term favourite reds which is now beginning to be a little overshadowed by the rest of the JS Portuguese red range.

Bairrada Reserva Aliança 1989   13 £B

Do Campo Tinto   14 £B

This rated 14 points over the summer of '93, it must be said,
and that rating must stand. It is no mean performer with its
gorgeous young beaujolais colour, feel and freshness; however, I have a hunch the wine will quickly develop even more
depth and flavour, and style, and by the time this book comes
out will be a considerably broader, deeper and even softer
wine, rating higher. It is a bargain under £3.

Herdade de Santa Marta 1991   14 £C

Great style at a great price. The distinctive sweetness, in an
essentially dry wine, is genuine and fresh-fruity and makes the
wine perfect with all manner of well-flavoured foods from
spicy sausages to chilli con carne.

Quinta da Bacalhoa, Palmela 1989   13 £D

Dry, raisiny, touch of figs. Typical Portuguese style.

PORTUGUESE WINE – *white*

Borba (Sainsbury's)   13 £B

Good fruit, good value.

Do Campo Branco   15 £B

A Peter Bright special for Sainsbury's (see *tinto* version also).
A delightfully fresh and fruity wine in the modern manner,
with an extended lush melony middle (prior to the wine
gushing down the throat and showing its lovely acidic zip
which refreshes the palate for further glasses), a result of Mr
Bright allowing the wine to spend time resting on its lees –
that is, all the bits and bobs from the crushed grapes – an

acquaintanceship with which gives wine character and
fullness. It is an excellent bottle to enjoy by itself or with
shellfish or grilled fish.

João Pires, Terras do Sado 1992   14   £C
Delicious muscat elegance. Lovely aperitif or with complex
and saucy fish dishes.

Santa Sara 1992   14   £C
Has elegance and style, a nice touch of oak, and although dry
and keenly finished has a lot of well-muscled fruit.

ROMANIAN WINE – *red*

Romanian Pinot Noir   16   £B
Shrewd boozers appreciate the absurdity of forking out under
three quid for a pinot noir which has spent between three and
four years in barrel and emerged rich, aromatic, and quite
stunningly concentrated (and better endowed than many a red
burgundy costing five times as much). If the store redesigned
the off-putting pseudo-KGB label it would sell twice as well
as it does. (N.B. to JS Director of Label Design – I have a
cracking idea for this label which would help sell *three times* as
many bottles but this idea is only available for (1) A lifetime's
supply of this wine or (2) The money to buy a small vineyard
in the Côte d'Or. Thinking about it, however, I think I'll take
the first option.)

Romanian Cabernet Sauvignon 1985   15   £B
A lot of character, finesse and hugely attractive mature style
for a piddling sum of money.

ROMANIAN WINE – *white*

Romanian Sylvaner (Sainsbury's)   15   £B
Wonderfully woody, toasted sesame seed aroma, pleasant melony fruit, good fresh finish. A brilliant aperitif.

SLOVAKIAN WINE – *white*

Pinot Blanc   11   £B
Some slight suggestion of varietal character.

Rizling Vlasky   12   £B
Interesting touch of newly ironed trouser in the aroma. Party wine for good party members.

SOUTH AFRICAN WINE – *red*

Pinotage, Coastal Region (Sainsbury's)   15   £C
Screams with flavour and blackberry and cherry fruit. Has a delicious dry macaroon edge to it. Pinotage wines can offer a boiled-sweet taste but this example has a superb freshness and naturalness about the flavour. A delicious confection.

SOUTH AFRICAN WINE – *white*

Bellingham Chardonnay 1991   14 £D
Oaked lemons and melons, basically. Very full of itself and
daring, style-wise, to offer hints of a grand white burgundy
like Montrachet.

Bon Vallon Chardonnay 1992   16 £B
Made by Danie de Wet, this has so much elegance and class
for under a fiver it's shocking. How dare the man concoct
such fruity finesse from chardonnay grapes! Doesn't he
realize there are French chardonnay growers, south of Dijon,
who need all the sales they can get (at three and four times the
price of this) in order to keep their Mercedes on the road! I
would not advise Danie to go on holiday in France except
heavily disguised.

Chardonnay, Western Cape (Sainsbury's)   15 £B
Elegance and concentration. Superb! No vintage on the label
but it's a '92 all right and it's remarkable stuff for the money,
with a delicious touch of exotic fruit to the subtle butteriness
and fresh, lemony finish. It cries out to be drunk with rich
crustaceous dishes. Smashing wine for just over £3.

Chenin Blanc (Sainsbury's)   15 £B
Gets to be a fruitier bargain every vintage. Peardrops and
sticky toffee to finish – oodles of fruit and great with fish and
chips.

**Sauvignon Blanc 1992, Olifants River
(Sainsbury's)**   14 £B
Delicious. Grilled fish – meet thy maker!

South African Colombard, Swartland
(Sainsbury's)   14   £B
Superb. Delicious appetite tickler and fish and chip wine.

SPANISH WINE – *red*

El Conde Vino de Mesa (Sainsbury's)   15   £B
Declassified rioja. Interesting wine (and at this price, ridiculous) which has been used to season new barrels, for three to
six months, for grander wines which will spend years in them.
So: can't be sold as rioja but can be sold as wine. It has the
vanilla aroma and delightful soft fruit but not the hefty finish.
Remarkable value for rioja lovers and perfect with a leaf salad
topped with flash-grilled slices of chorizo.

La Mancha, Castillo de Alhambra
(Sainsbury's) 1992   15   £B
Spain's answer to beaujolais (but without beaujolais's price
and acidic freshness). Beautiful, bright, supple fruit, very drily
finished. Terrific value.

Marqués de Cáceres Rioja 1987 (1.5 litres)   14   £E
Great big bottle, big soft wine.

Navarra (Sainsbury's)   11   £B

Navarra Tempranillo/Cabernet Sauvignon
1990   15   £C
Brilliant classy wine of depth, character and style. Dry, fruity,
very mouth-puckering. Good value for this level of rich
oomph.

**Rioja Crianza, Bodegas Olarra 1989
(Sainsbury's)**   14   £C

Rioja (Sainsbury's)   14   £B
Superb light rioja of excellent fruit and flavour.

Torres Gran Coronas Reserva 1987   14   £E

Utiel-Requena 1988 (Sainsbury's)   12   £B

Valencia Red (Sainsbury's)   13   £B
Excellent value for pizzas.

**Viña Herminia Reserva Rioja, Bodegas
Lagunilla 1985**   14   £D
Lush, raunchy stuff – delicious cheese wine.

SPANISH WINE – *white and rosé*

Castillo de Alhambra Rosé 1992   14   £B
Rosado Garnacho. Typical cherry nose, pink complexion and
dry sense of humour. An amusing clown of a wine.

Dry White   10   £A

La Mancha (Sainsbury's)   13   £A

Moscatel de Valencia (Sainsbury's)   16   £B
Brilliant honeyed wine with a finish like marmalade. Superb
pudding wine for a song.

Moscatel Pale Cream Sherry   16   £C
The history of the world, indeed the history of food and wine,
is full of great discoveries made by happy accident. But for
America and Russia bickering about space we wouldn't have

non-stick saucepans. But for a drop of oil creeping surrep-
titiously and serendipitously into an egg yolk mayonnaise
would be undreamed of. Then there's wine itself. 5000 years
ago someone or other scooped up the liquid left by a bunch of
mouldering grapes ignored by everybody else and felt heady
and excited because he or she was drinking alcohol created by
the yeast on the skins eating the sugar in the fruit. And now
we have Sainsbury's Moscatel Pale Cream Sherry which the
store developed last year in Jerez in order, one must assume,
to bring a bit of added excitement to vicars' at-home after-
noons and geriatric bridge parties since who else but the
honey-dentured drink such sickly stuff? However, Sainsbury's
motives in attempting to spice up the sweet sherry market with
a previously unheard-of marriage between the moscatel grape
and the palomino grape which makes sherry are insignificant
beside the true role of this new tipple. By complete accident,
J. Sainsbury has created the world's first ice-cream wine.
Well-chilled Moscatel Pale Cream Sherry is the best thing
with ice-cream I've ever tasted. The musky, melony quality of
muscat is balanced brilliantly by the saccharine nutty flavour
of the sherry and helped by a high alcohol content (17%).

Navarra Viura-chardonnay 1992 (Sainsbury's)   14   £C
Lots of good fruit, freshness and style. Good value.

Rioja Blanco, Bodega Olarra (Sainsbury's)   14   £B
Banana-soft fruit, pineapple-tinged. Typical, delicious and
very good value.

Rueda Sauvignon Blanc 1992   14   £C
Certainly the wackiest sauvignon blanc I've set lips to in a long
time. A ridiculously frivolous, frilly-skirted wine which giggles
rather than guffaws with fruit. And so exotic and perfumed a
strumpet could stick it behind her ears.

Torres Viña Sol 1992   12   £C

Valdepeñas Blanco (Sainsbury's)   15   £A
Terrific two quid wine. The airén, picked early from well-
sited vineyards on limestone soil, and then lovingly vinified to
give a modern melon/lemon balance, and overall classy feel,
makes a mockery of this grape's rotten reputation.

USA WINE – *red*

**Beaulieu Vineyards Beautout Cabernet
Sauvignon 1988**   13   £D
Has an elegant creamy texture of some attraction.

La Crema 1988   17   £C
First the good news: this wine has the classic pinot aroma of
truffles and well-hung grouse plus a savoury edge to the
raspberry and blackberry fruit. It's a Pavarotti of a pinot: deep,
fat, lingering. It is not unknown for Americans to turn out
interesting pinots noirs but I have never tasted one this richly
wonderful for less than £30. To Mr Gregory Graziano of
Sebastopol, California, who made this wine, my congratula-
tions and my best wishes for a speedy recovery from the
effects of the thumbscrews the Sainsbury buyer presumably
used to extract the wine from you at such a piddling price.
Now the bad news: this wine may be all gone by the time you
thumb these pages; reinforcements have been promised but
these too may be quickly exhausted. I don't want to raise your
hopes too high but I had to let you in on this wine if at all
possible.

USA WINE – *white and rosé*

California Chardonnay (Sainsbury's)   13   £C

California White Zinfandel (Sainsbury's)   13   £C
A marvellous rosé intro to wine for scholars and other layabouts who lead sheltered unproductive lives but occasionally emerge to have fun. This is a rosé wine in spite of being called white (that's California for you).

Firestone Chardonnay, Santa Ynez 1991   15   £E
Californian chic. Beautifully elegant wine.

Sauvignon Blanc, Firestone 1991 (Sainsbury's)   11   £C

**Sauvignon Blanc, Washington State 1991
(Sainsbury's)**   12   £C

SPARKLING WINE/CHAMPAGNE

Australian Sparkling Wine (Sainsbury's)   14   £C
Excellent stuff for cheap wedding givers.

Cava (Sainsbury's)   15   £C
A delicious, earth-edged cava. Quite delicious drinking for under a fiver.

Champagne Extra Dry (Sainsbury's)   14   £F
Good at the price; lovely biscuity fruit and dry with it. So much better than the famous marques for so much less money.

Champagne Rosé (Sainsbury's)   13   £F

Clairette de Die (Sainsbury's)   13   £D
Fondant cream peaches – very amusing aperitif.

Crémant de Bourgogne Rosé (Sainsbury's)   14   £D
Terrific blusher for the money.

Cuvée Napa, Mumm California   13   £E
Quiet, not explosive, and rather like a reasonably made
champagne.

**Green Point Vineyard Domaine Chandon 1990
Australia**   13   £E
Under a tenner, a restraint which stretches to the fruit but this
is certainly better than many champagnes at twice the price.

**Jeanmaire Champagne Blanc de Blancs Grand
Cru 1988**   13   £E
Light style. A very posh aperitif.

Mercier Champagne   11   £F

Moscato d'Asti   14   £B
A terrific 5.5% alcohol semi-sparkling sweetie for old folks
any time, young folks at christenings and bar-mitzvahs, and
middle-aged fogies with a soft heart to appreciate it and a
hard fruit tart to eat alongside it. Has hints of oranges, lemons
and face-powder.

Salinger Brut 1989   14   £E
Very lemony, light, and very elegant. Good under-a-tenner
celebration sparkler.

Saumur (Sainsbury's)   14   £D
Bargain. Pleasant dry fruit of some distinction for the price.

Vintage Champagne Blanc de Blancs 1988
(Sainsbury's)   14   £G

Excellent. This is the lighter style, which some drinkers feel is more elegant, and certainly this is a bottle one can drain rather than sip nervously.

Vouvray (Sainsbury's)   14   £D

Yalumba Pinot Noir/Chardonnay, Australia   16   £E

Absolute stunner for the money: rich and biscuity, great balancing acidity and an overall style hinting at refinement and class. Rheims quakes in its Gucci boots!

Tesco

De gustibus non est disputandum, as some old Latin geezer said, and by golly didn't he hit the nail on the head? I scratch my glabrous forepate in wonderment at how it can be that Tesco manage to sell 60,000 bottles a year of Keo, the store's Cyprus red. This wine is as near undrinkable as a wine can be, though it might form the basis of a wacky vinaigrette. It must be nostalgia (appropriately from the Greek *nostos*, return home, and *algia*, pain) on the part of the Cypriot community, for only those who grew up with such a wine could take it to their bosom let alone their lips. This cautionary tale tells the supermarket sleuth much about the nature of the supermarket with the biggest wine list of all. Its larger stores offer 780 bottles of wine, more than any other supermarket by far. (Sainsbury's, for example, has 300-odd wines, Safeway some 400.)

Tesco is not content to cater for one end of the market, like Morrisons say, or the other, like Waitrose, and it doesn't seem to wish to settle for the middle like, for example, Sainsbury's. No, Tesco wants the whole damn caboodle. It's unhappy to think there's a drinker alive who can't find what he or she wants on a Tesco wine shelf, be they a homesick Mediterranean, a once-a-month Lambrusco tippler, or a sophisticated sipper of expensive clarets (Les Forts de Latour 1985, £26) and white burgundies (Delauney's Puligny Montrachet 1985, £22). Funny year, '85.

It was also a funny year when I holidayed in Cornwall and, in much the same spirit as families visit Disneyland, took the children to the large Tesco I knew to be in Truro. My object was the store's 14-point chianti which, for just over three quid the bottle, I knew would provide me with days of happy cheap fruity glugging. Imagine my disappointment, then, when upon reaching the chianti shelf it was empty. I peered closer, hoping to find a bottle lurking in the depths of the shelving. There was nothing but a vast empty hole where scores of bottles of this delectable chianti once stood. Then a ticket, affixed to the edge of the shelf, caught my eye. It said words to the effect of: '*Superplonk of the* Guardian *says this wine is brilliant.*' I was hoist, wineless, by my very own praise. But things got worse. I turned to the man filling an adjacent shelf with wine and indicated the vast empty chianti space.

'Nothing like a recommendation from a decent newspaper to shift wine, eh?' I said cheerfully.

The shelf filler looked at me as if I was barking. 'Don't make me laugh,' he said. 'That wine's been on special offer all week. S'gone like hot cakes.'

I slunk away, children in either hand my only comfort, but I was easily able to find other chiantis at the same store, for Tesco isn't only the supermarket which caters for everyone – it also doesn't stop short, as do its competitors, at just one or two representatives of a particular region's wines. Oh no. Whereas Sainsbury's, say, is content with four chiantis and Safeway with three, Tesco piles it high with nine. A short while back they stocked no fewer than 50 champagnes (or rather a few of their larger stores did) and this put them ahead of their competitors. However, the range has now shrunk to exactly half this number and the likes of Pol Roger Cuvée Winston Churchill at £40 have gone, although the 1982 Dom Pérignon still hangs in there even though it's a tenner more expensive (£55) than it was in Tesco five years ago. It's a rare supermarket wine which is still on sale after five years and I dare say, unless the directors do the decent thing and put Dom out of its misery and polish it off themselves, it'll still be on sale well into the next century. At the inflation rate Tesco lumber it with, by the year 2050 it'll sport a £169 price tag and, if the recession is over by then, some loony squandermaniac is sure to buy it.

Most Tesco customers, of course, put up with rather gentler price tags. The store has been in the front trench of the battle to keep the £1.99 bottle alive and well and hardly a month goes by when the store hasn't a cute red and white pair going for a song.

Tesco is always keen to steal a march on its competitors (and with its purchase of the Catteau chain in northern France it can be said to have stolen 92 marches) but in the end it likes to believe it's cheaper than anyone else. The store's head of wine buying, Stephen Clarke, insists: 'The regular competitive buying checks we carry out show that we've been cheaper than anyone else during this recession, for we've taken the view that we must keep wine drinkers, even the light one bottle a week drinkers, in the market for wine rather than see them give up drinking it altogether.' I like this sentiment. I think it's good there's so much concern at Tesco for us tipplers. In the end it's our pockets which will feel the benefits.

ARGENTINIAN WINE – *red*

Cabernet Sauvignon (Tesco)	12	£A
Mendoza Malbec 1992, International Winemaker Series	12	£B
Trapiche Pinot Noir Reserve 1988	14	£C

Uvas del Sol Argentinian Red 13 £B
Hairy and well-muscled with fruit so mouth-filling you need
food to help you chew your way through it.

Uvas del Sol Malbec/Cabernet Sauvignon 13 £C
My God, this is rich. Unique style of fruit I've not encoun-
tered before. Has a wonderful alien feel as if it was made on
Mars. Brilliant with a spicy pizza.

ARGENTINIAN WINE – *white*

Argentinian White 1991 (Tesco) 11 £A

**Mendoza Blanc 1992, International
Winemaker Series** 13 £B
One of the best of this series of Tesco's wines but scored
more highly when it was younger and fresher.

Trapiche Chardonnay 1991 13 £C

Uvas del Sol Chardonnay 1993 13 £C
Rich, forward fruit. Needs fish soup.

Uvas del Sol Torrontes 12 £C
Curious, very curious. Celery-flavoured fruit! Attractive
aperitif.

Uvas del Sol Vino Fino Blanco 1992 12 £B

AUSTRALIAN WINE – *red*

Barramundi Shiraz/Merlot   14   £C
Vibrant, spicy, fun.

Cabernet Sauvignon (Tesco)   13   £C
Lovely cuddly soft fruit. Very tongue-huggable.

Cabernet Sauvignon/Shiraz (Tesco)   14   £C

Coonawarra Cabernet Sauvignon 1990 (Tesco)   15   £D
A refined, quite bookish Aussie – like encountering Crocodile
Dundee reading Dante in the original. Lots of fruit yet elegant
with it.

Orlando RF Cabernet Sauvignon 1990   14   £C

Penfolds Bin 707 Cabernet Sauvignon 1989   14   £G
You need to be well-heeled to enjoy this wine's embrace and
well-lipped to survive it.

**Pinot Noir Merlot 1992, International
Winemaker Series**   13   £C
Attractive cherry and plum wine. Good with pastas etc.

Ryecroft McLaren Vale Belltrees Merlot 1991   15   £C
Barrel-chested and even a mite violent yet parades senti-
mental touches in the manner of a muscled knucklehead
tattooed with 'Mother' and 'Fido, I love you'. This wine has
lots of sweat and savouriness to its fruit, is soft and new-
leathery, and has a soft chocolate centre.

St Halletts Old Block Shiraz, Barossa 1990   14   £E
Mint but no hole in this fruit. Only at a few Tescos.

Shiraz (Tesco) 13 £C
Excellent value, demurely fruity.

**South Australia Shiraz/Cabernet Sauvignon
(Tesco)** 14 £B
Brilliant value. The shiraz and cabernet sauvignon grape
varieties combine most attractively and offer a tarry aroma,
excellent fruit with some cherry and plum, and a dryness
which is not too spicy or sweaty. Outstanding value.

Yalumba Shiraz 1990 13 £C

AUSTRALIAN WINE – *white*

Australian White (Tesco) 12 £B
Twenty years ago this wine would have labelled itself Australian hock.

Barramundi Semillon/Chardonnay 15 £C
This wine gets better and better every bottle I taste. Full and
orchideaceous, woody and warm, it bursts with buttered bananas, vanilla, peaches and ice-cream yet also possesses
refreshing balancing acidity. Great glugging stuff.

Chardonnay (Tesco) 12 £C

Colombard/Chardonnay 1992 (Tesco) 14 £B
A diet of fruit this rich would keep you very healthy.

Fumé Blanc Hunter Valley, Rosemount 1992 13 £D

Houghton Wildflower Ridge Chenin Blanc 1991 13 £C

McLaren Vale Chardonnay 1991 (Tesco) 14 £D
Snazzy, jazzy fruit with vanilla/banana touches. Good acidity

to this richness makes this a more complete style of Aussie chardonnay. Very attractive.

Moondah Brook Verdelho 1990	13	£C

Preece Chardonnay 1991	12	£D

Rhine Riesling (Tesco) 15 £B
Rich, oily and most attractively fruity. Great aperitif and also with fish. Interesting accompaniment to complex salads.

Sauvignon Blanc (Tesco)	13	£C

Semillon (Tesco)	12	£B

Semillon/Chardonnay Penfolds 1992	13	£C

**Semillon/Riesling 1992, International
Winemaker Series** 10 £C

Western Australian Chenin Blanc (Tesco) 14 £C
Lemons, clementines, lots of flavoursome gooseberries and even a touch of flinty lychee – can this be a wine, I ask myself, or a fruit salad? It's a smashing tipple.

**Yalumba Museum Show Reserve Rutherglen
Muscat (half)** 14 £D
Considering you get cough mixture, floor polish, oranges, cherries and herbal honey in your glass, the fact that the stuff in the glass has cost you £2.30 is probably a fair price. But it is an acquired taste – and strictly for deep rich desserts and deep rich pockets. (Adventurous souls, seeking perfumed feet, could try polishing up the floorboards with it.)

AUSTRIAN WINE – *red*

Winzerhaus Blauer Zweigelt 1991   15   £C
Joyously drinkable. (Try it chilled.) Like a summer pudding
swirling in the glass. Yet it's not sweet but bramble-dry and
the crushed berried fruit has a slight new leather feel to it.
The '92 vintage is not yet to hand, or glass, as I write but I
dare say it'll be every bit as good – if it isn't I shall be surprised
and disappointed as this is one of my favourite wines.

AUSTRIAN WINE – *white*

Austrian Dry White   14   £B
Lovely pear, apple and peach fruit and controlled acidity.
Quite delicious and superb value for money.

Winzerhaus Grüner Veltliner 1991   16   £B
This vintage has opened up, the fruit deepened, the acidity
developed, and this mélange of green grass, wet wool, cob
nuts and raspberries has become, drunk in the late summer, a
considerably stylish wine rather than a merely deliciously
slurpable one.

Winzerhaus Pinot Blanc 1991   13   £B

Winzerhaus Welschriesling 1991   13   £B

BULGARIAN WINE – *red*

Bulgarian Country Red	13	£B
Cabernet Sauvignon Reserve (Tesco)	12	£B

Good fruit.

BULGARIAN WINE – *white*

Bulgarian Country White	12	£A
Chardonnay Reserve 1990 (Tesco)	12	£B

Under three quid bargain.

CHILEAN WINE – *red*

Chilean Cabernet Sauvignon (Tesco)   13   £B

Chilean Red Mondragón (Tesco)   13   £B
Excellent price for a well-structured wine.

Cousino Macul Merlot 1989   14   £C

Merlot (Tesco)   13   £B
Whiff of stalky typicality to the attractive dark cherry fruit, slightly chocolaty. Excellent with roast meat nosh-ups.

Montes Alpha, Cabernet Sauvignon 1988   14   £E

Casablanca Chardonnay Santa Rita 1992   14   £D
Has elegance and haute couture cut. Even so, it's not afraid to be very, very fruity.

CHILEAN WINE – *white*

Chardonnay 1991 (Tesco)	13	£C

Chilean White Mondragón 1992 (Tesco)　　　14　£B
A lot of happy fruit. Sane, smiling, balanced – and that's
merely the way drinkers of this bargain feel about the state of
their finances.

Sauvignon Blanc Santa Rita 1991	14	£B
Villard Chardonnay 1990	12	£C
Villard Sauvignon Blanc 1991	11	£C

CYPRIOT WINE – *red*

Keo Othello	4	£B

CYPRIOT WINE – *white*

Keo Aphrodite Dry White	11	£B

CZECH WINE – *red*

Slovakian Country Red (Tesco) (litre)	10	£C

ENGLISH WINE – *white*

English Table Wine 1990   14   £B
Fit for anyone's table. Keen grassy nose (summoning up
images of sticky wickets and cries of 'howzat?'), an amusing
dose of real fruit and a finish hinting at Kent cob nuts. This
latter hint is no surprise since the wine is grown in the Kent's
High Weald. Good price.

Southern Counties Quality Wine   14   £C
Possibly the ugliest name ever put to a wine. The advertising
industry ruined the word 'quality' fifty years ago and it's been
buried in Little Splendour ever since. What a pity! This is a
most attractive Berkshire wine, fresh and well-structured and
excellent with shellfish. It's a credit to its maker John
Woronstchak. But whoever thought of that name – which is
largely based on new EC regulations regarding English wine
nomenclature – should be hung and drawn and his remains
used to fertilize the vineyard (if it would have him).

FRENCH WINE – *red*

Beaujolais (Tesco)   11   £C

Bourgueil, Domaine Hubert, La Huralaie 1990 15   £D
A red to try chilled for its raspberry fruit has a dry, mineral
edge which can be likened to licking the end of a lead pencil
and if drunk too warm the subtlety of this can be marred.
Utterly sublime, I think it.

Burgundy, Henri de Bahezre (Tesco)   12   £C

Buzet, Domaine de la Croix 1989 12 £C

**Cabernet Sauvignon Haute Vallée de l'Aude
(Tesco)** 13 £B
Excellent value for the family get-together with a roast on the
table.

Château Bois Galant Médoc 1988 13 £D

Château Cantemerle Haut-Médoc 1987 13 £F

Château d'Arsac Haut-Médoc 1990 12 £G

Château de Camensac Haut-Médoc 1988 13 £E

Château de Caraguilhes 1989 14 £C
An organic wine from Corbières which has been consistently
rich and earthy, and very good value, for several vintages now.
However, I am concerned to see this wine sticking out its head
close to the £4.50 bench mark where the Australian barrage is
mightiest and thus I fear for its survival at this price.

Château des Gondats Bordeaux Superieur 1989 13 £C

Château du Bluizard Beaujolais Villages 1991 11 £C

Château Léon Premières Côtes de Bordeaux 12 £C

Château les Gravières St-Emilion 1988 14 £E
Delicious, soft, very supple.

Château Marquis-de-Terme Margaux 1988 13 £E
There is a touch of beefiness about this grand Margaux but I
would prefer to wait a few years before I met it and it had
softened.

Château Pigoudet, Coteaux d'Aix en Provence
1988   14   £C
Sunny (and pretty) Provence in a bottle, plus a touch of Côtes
du Rhone earthiness. Excellent drinking.

Château St-Georges St-Emilion 1986   13   £G

Château St-Nicholas, Fronsac 1987   10   £D

Château Toutigeac Bordeaux 1991   13   £C

Châteauneuf-du-Pape, Les Arnevels 1990   14   £D
Meaty, rich, well-muscled. A classy dollop of fruit.

Chinon, Baronnies Madeleine 1986   14   £D
Rabelais said of wine like this that it slid down the throat 'like
taffeta'. I can't improve on that.

Claret (Tesco)   13   £B

Clos de Chenoves, Buxy 1988   13   £D

Côtes de Provence (Tesco)   12   £B

Côtes de Roussillon (Tesco)   12   £B

Côtes de Duras 1989   11   £B

Côtes du Frontonnais 1990   13   £B

Côtes du Rhône (Tesco)   12   £B

Côtes du Rhône Villages 1992   12   £C

Crozes-Hermitage, Domaine Cécile Mussel
1990   11   £F

Domaine Beaulieu St-Saveur, Marmandais
1990   12   £B

Domaine de Beaufort, Minervois 1991	13	£B
Domaine de Conroy, Brouilly 1991	11	£D
Domaine des Baumelles, Côtes du Luberon 1991	13	£C
Domaine les Hauts des Chambert, Cahors 1988	13	£D
Dorgan, Vin de Pays de l'Aude (Tesco)	13	£B
Escoubes, Vin de Pays des Côtes de Gascogne	12	£B
Fitou (Tesco)	11	£B
French Country Cabernet Sauvignon, Vin de Pays de la Haute Vallée de l'Aude (Tesco)	12	£B
French Country Red (Tesco) (1 litre)	13	£C
Gévrey Chambertin Marchand 1988	13	£F
Grand Carat, Vin de Pays du Comte Tolosan 1991	10	£B

Grenache, Vin de Pays d'Oc 1992 (Tesco) 13 £B
Excellent fruit.

Hautes Côtes de Nuits, Caves des Hautes Côtes 1989	11	£D
Hautes Côtes du Beaune, Caves de Hautes Côtes 1990	12	£D

La Vieille Ferme Reserve, Côtes du Rhone 1990 16 £C
Easily the best branded red wine I have ever tasted. (La Vieille
Ferme is not a vineyard, as you might not unreasonably think,
it is a brand name). It liberally coats the tongue in lashings of
soft fruit to give the feel of crystallized velvet.

Les Forts de Latour, Pauillac 1985   11 £H
Doesn't take anywhere near so long to reach maturity as its
world-famous relative but it's still got a way to go. But do you
want to wait? Equally, do you want to spend nigh on thirty
quid on a wine which had been on the shelf goodness knows
how long? At a wine merchant, fine wine can be stored
properly and remain unsold and in good nick for years, but
how can this be matched in a supermarket? Even if the bottle
isn't completely upright it's inclined sufficiently for the label
to be read and so the cork is not completely covered by the
wine and it may shrink and permit oxidation to occur. I would
be happier to see fine wines like this, leaving aside the argu-
ment that this *soi-disant* example may not be remotely worth
the money, being adequately cellared and available for order
with one bottle being displayed on shelf for customers to see
but not buy. I do not see how '85 Pauillacs can be sold off the
shelf in the same way as a £3 Australian bottle which only sits
around for a few weeks at most.

Les Terres Fines Syrah, Vin de Pays de l'Hérault		
1990	11	£B

Margaux 1989 (Tesco)	11	£E

Médoc (Tesco)	11	£C

Merlot, Vin de Pays de la Haute Vallée de l'Aude
(Tesco)   13 £B
Don't put pepper on your sausages. Drink this wine with them
instead.

Morgon, Arthur Barolet 1991	12	£D

Pauillac 1988 (Tesco)	11	£D

Pavillon Rouge du Château Margaux 1989	12	£G

St-Emilion (Tesco)	12	£C
St-Joseph 1989	10	£C
Saumur Champigny 1991	13	£D
Savigny les Beaune, Hospices de Beaune 1986	12	£F
Syrah, Vin de Pays des Collines Rhodaniennes	13	£B
Vin de Pays de la Cité de Carcassonne 1990	12	£B
Vin de Pays de la Gironde 1992 (Tesco)	11	£B
Vin de Pays de Pérignan 1992	13	£B
Vin de Pays des Côtes de Gascogne, Yvon Mau	11	£A

FRENCH WINE – *white and rosé*

Alsace Gewürztraminer 1991 (Tesco)	11	£D
Alsace Pinot Blanc (Tesco)	10	£B
Alsace Riesling 1991 (Tesco)	11	£C
Beaujolais Blanc 1991	11	£C
Blayais	10	£B
Cabernet de Saumur, Caves des Vignerons de Saumur Rosé 1990	13	£B

Cabernet Sauvignon Blanc de Noirs, Vin de Pays de l'Aude, International Winemaker Series 15 £C
Faintest suggestion of a blush – as might visit the cheek of a saint who has overheard an obscene joke. Rich aroma and

flavour, good deep fruit, melon and subtle peardrop, good finish. Delicious aperitif.

Cépage Terret, Vin de Pays de l'Herault, Delta Domaines 1991   13   £B

Chablis 1992 (Tesco)   12   £D

Chablis Premier Cru, Montmain, La Chablisienne 1989   14   £E

Chablis La Chablisienne 1991 (Tesco)   12   £D

Chardonnay, Vin de Pays d'Oc (Tesco)   11   £B

Chasan 1991, International Winemaker Series   12 . £B
Some pleasant melon fruit to this Vin de Pays d'Oc.

Château de Carles Sauternes 1990   13   £F
A rich dessert wine, or aperitif if you will (and I will with pleasure, thank you) which I find somewhat expensive. It would repay cellaring – for a decade.

Château La Forêt-St-Hilaire, Entre-Deux-Mers 1990   12   £C

Château les Girotins, Sauternes 1989 (half)   13   £D
Succulence and sweetness in a handy size.

Château Magneau, Graves 1990   13   £E

Château Malagar, Bordeaux Blanc 1990   15   £C
A delicious wine of fruit and nuts. Distinguished in feel, grand in effect, and superb with grilled sole.

Château Vert Bois 1991   13   £C

Châteauneuf-du-Pape, Les Arnevels, Quiot
1991   14 £D
A bottle of this and a fresh grilled river trout and you could
become delirious with joy.

Côtes de Provence (Tesco)   11 £B

Côtes de Roussillon (Tesco)   12 £B
Some pleasant fruit to this.

Cuvée Reserve Côtes du Rhône Blanc   15 £C
Tesco takes over the 100 per cent bourboulenc (grape variety)
crown from Safeway. This is an unusual wine, unusually
beautifully balanced, unusually good value for a Rhône white,
and most unusual of all, it's on sale in Britain. Undoubtedly,
the winemaker's New World experience has helped for this is
a modern wine, without being horribly tarty and obviously
fruity, and very stylish with aroma, finish and class. Great with
trout or salmon.

Domaine de Jalousie, Vin de Pays des Côtes de
Gascogne, Late Harvest 1990   12 £C
Late harvest denotes not tardiness but deliberately allowing
the grapes to ripen past the time they might normally be
picked for vinification. Thus, this wine demonstrates a rich
side. Personally, I think it best before eating rather than after.

Domaine du Bois Chardonnay, Vin de Pays
d'Oc 1992   15 £C
Almonds and rich fruit combine here to most compelling
effect. Great value. Of great interest to fish lovers (salmon
grilled or poached).

Domaine St-Alain, Vin de Pays des Côtes
du Tarn   12 £B
Attractive, melony fruit.

Domaine Saubagnère 1992 (Tesco)   15 £C
Smackeroony of a mouth-filler! Swirling fruit flavours including melon, orange and pineapple. Yet not overpowering or
yukky. Great stuff!

**Dry Muscat, Vin de Pays des Pyrénées-
Orientales 1992**   12 £B
Library pong, sour nose – excellent for live mollusc con-
sumption.

Entre-Deux-Mers (Tesco)   12 £B

**Escoubes, Vin de Pays des Côtes des
Gascogne (Tesco)**   12 £B

Floc de Gascogne   14 £D
Made from grape juice with armagnac tossed in to bring it up
to 17%. A simple peasant recipe and I enjoy its rusticity as a
pick-me-up (or should I say as a pull-me-down?) after a hard
day's wine tasting. The view of my household is that it is about
as toothsome a proposition as old rugby boots pickled in
treacle.

**French Country White, Côtes de Gascogne
(Tesco)**   13 £C
Clean and melony.

Graves (Tesco)   13 £C
Excellent fish wine.

Les Terres Fines, Muscat Sec 1990   12 £C

Mâcon Blanc Villages 1991 (Tesco)   11 £C

**Menetou-Salon, Domaine de la Montaloise
1990**   12 £C

Miribeau, Vin des Pays d'Oc Sur Lie 1991	12	£B
Monbazillac (Tesco)	12	£C
Muscadet Sur Lie, Domaine de la Huperie 1991	12	£C
Muscat Cuvée José Sala	15	£C

Toffee-nosed and less than £4? Aristocratic sweetness never came so cheap.

Pouilly-Fumé, Cuvée Jules 1990	11	£D
Premières Côtes de Bordeaux (Tesco)	11	£B
St-Romain, Arthur Barolet 1988	13	£E
Sancerre Alphonse Mellot 1991	11	£E
Sauvignon Blanc Bordeaux (Tesco)	13	£B
Vin de Pays de la Dordogne, Sigoules	12	£B
Vin des Pays des Côtes du Tarn	11	£B

GERMAN WINE – *red*

Baden Pinot Noir 1990	12	£C

Has a cough-sweet quality you may find useful in darkest mid-winter.

GERMAN WINE – *white*

Baden Dry	13	£B

Sound value to be had here.

Bereich Johannisberg, Riesling, Krayer 1991	12	£C
Bernkasteler Kurfurstlay	13	£B
Dry Country German Wine (1 litre)	13	£C
Dry Hock	13	£B

Fresh and straightforward and good with fish dishes.

Grans Fassian, Riesling Trocken 1990	13	£D

The taste buds will emerge from this exquisite citric dousing quivering for food.

Guldentaler Riesling Auslese 1989	14	£C

Lemon and eau de cologne. Delightful but searing.

Hock (Tesco)	11	£A
Morio Muskat	12	£A

Good grapey thirst quencher.

Mosel Medium Dry Riesling (Tesco)	11	£B
Niersteiner Gutes Domtal	12	£A
Niersteiner Pettenthal Riesling Spâtlese Balbach 1989	13	£C
Piesporter Treppchen Riesling Kabinett 1991	12	£C
Rauenthaler Rothenberg Riesling Kabinett 1989	12	£C
Rheinpfalz Dry Riesling	12	£B
Rheinpfalz Medium Dry Silvaner	11	£B
Ruppertsberger Hohenberg Riesling Kabinett 1989	13	£C

St Johanner Abtei Kabinett (Tesco)	11	£B
St Johanner Abtei Spätlese (Tesco)	12	£B

Scharzhofberger Van Volxem 1990 13 £C
A delicious silky aperitif.

**Steinweiler Kloster Liebfrauenberg Auslese
(Tesco)** 12 £C

**Steinweiler Kloster Liefrauenberg Kabinett
(Tesco)** 10 £B

**Steinweiler Kloster Liebrauenberg Spätlese
(Tesco)** 11 £C

Stettener Stein, Franken 1989 11 £C
I dare say a bottle would be quite acceptable with a plate of
raw oysters.

Weissburgunder Rietburg 1991 12 £B

GREEK WINE – *red*

Nemea 1990 12 £C
Those with a classical leaning may be amused to drink a wine
to which Agamemnon was partial.

GREEK WINE – *white*

Kretikos 1991 12 £C

HUNGARIAN WINE – *red*

Hungarian Table Wine 1991 (Tesco) (1 litre)   11   £B
If you fancy being swiped in the kisser by a bunch of soggy
dandelions then here's a welcoming bouquet you'll really
enjoy. But there is some fruit of a pleasanter disposition.

HUNGARIAN WINE – *white*

Hungarian Chardonnay 1991 (Tesco)   11   £B

ITALIAN WINE – *red*

Barbaresco 1987 (Tesco)   12   £D

Barolo, Giacosa Fratelli 1987   13   £D

Cabernet Sauvignon del Veneto   15   £B
I had a thoroughly fruity experience with this wine, which is so
up-front with its blackcurrant jam-juicy fruit, balanced by a
vivid acidity which keeps you coming back for yet another
glass, that I whistled through a bottle during one episode of
Coronation Street. Terrific value for under three quid and
you'll recognize it in store by its unholy mess of a label which
sports purplish line drawings of cobweb-bedecked curlicue
plinths and columns on a reddish background.

Carmignano Capezzano 1987   16   £C
Blackcurrants and raspberries underlie an aroma of cooked

figs. Superb wine of exceptional complexity and depth for the money. Indeed, so cheap is it for the class of wine it is that I'm not sure the Tesco employee who sticks the prices on hasn't made a huge mistake. Like finding an old Bentley in show-room condition with a nought knocked off.

Chianti 1991 (Tesco) 14 £B
Easily one of the best chiantis around for value for money.

Chianti Classico 1990 (Tesco) 14 £C
Delicious. Typical aroma and taste with all the earthy, firm, teeth-puckering fruit of the sangiovese grape.

Chianti Classico Riserva 1988 (Tesco) 13 £D
Excellent style but a touch pricey.

Chianti Colli Senesi (Tesco) 13 £C
Attractive, warm, terra cotta finish.

Chianti Rufina 1990 Grati (Tesco) 13 £C

Chianti Rufina, Villa di Monte 1985 12 £B
Under £3.50 for an 8-year-old? Remarkable.

Dolcetto d'Acqui 1990 (Tesco) 15 £B
Mouthwateringly good value. A delicious, sweet-natured, cheering wine of soothing acidity and lovely gushing fruit, arm-flinging and expressive. Yummy.

Merlot del Piave 11 £B

Montelpulciano d'Abruzzo (Tesco) 12 £B

Montepulciano d'Abruzzo, Bianchi 1991 13 £B

Orfeno dell'Uccellina 1990 13 £B
An excellent price for some good fruit.

Pinot Noir del Veneto (Tesco)   12   £B
Rich little aroma, fresh raspberry acid. Cool it and enjoy.

Ripa della Mandorle 1990   13   £D

Rosso Rubino   13   £B

Sicilian Red (Tesco)   13   £B
Also comes in a useful 3-litre box for under £11 (equalling
45p a glass).

Villa Boscorotondo Chianti Classico 1990   14   £C
Very individual wine made by John Matta in the heart of
Chiantishire. Rather less assertive than the norm but no less
attractive: soft, gently earthy, nutty fruit finish.

Villa Pigna Rosso Piceno 1992   13   £B
Delicious soft fruit with a dryish background and a rich edge.

ITALIAN WINE – *white*

**Basilicata Bianco 1992, International
Winemaker Series**   10   £B

Chardonnay Alto Adige, Von Keller 1991   14   £C
Von Keller's chardonnays are always interesting and, at under
£4, good value.

Chardonnay del Veneto (Tesco)   12   £B

Colli Albani 1992 (Tesco)   12   £B

Colli Toscani 1992 (Tesco)   12   £B

Cormons Isonzo Pinot Bianco 1992   13   £C
Vivid fruit. Most attractive rich style.

Frascati 1991 (Tesco)	12	£B
Gambellara Monte Bocara 1990	13	£B
Locorotondo	12	£B
Naragus 1990	13	£B
Orvieto Classico Vaselli 1991	12	£B
Pinot Grigio del Veneto (Tesco)	13	£B
Pinot Grigio Tiefenbrunner 1990	13	£C
Sicilian White (Tesco)	13	£B
Soave Classico 1991 (Tesco)	12	£B

Terre di Ginestra 1991 13 £C
Cataratto is the grape variety which makes this wine and there is nothing catty or ratty about it.

Terre Toscano 1991 (Tesco) 12 £B

Verdicchio Classico, Villa Bianchi 1991 13 £C
An excellent example of the breed: nicely balanced, fresh and crisp, fruity and nutty.

Vespaiolo Breganze Villa Magna 1990 13 £C
Extraordinary wine of such lush lime, keen-edgedness that it fair takes your breath away. It has a bitter almond undertone which doesn't entirely gell with the fruit and the overall effect is of a wine at war with itself – rather like those Italian marriages seen on the big screen with one party throwing hard objects at the other party and narrowly missing.

MEXICAN WINE – *red*

Cabernet Sauvignon 1988 (Tesco)   14   £C
Fine style from L. A. Cetto. Burnt toffeed fruit (plum and
blackberry). Has strata of flavour and texture to its fruit from
denim to silk. Under four quid, it's a snip.

NEW ZEALAND WINE – *red*

Cabernet Sauvignon 1990 (Tesco)   14   £C
The fruit's all there, but the bouquet's a bit barking: smells
like a lawnmower grassbox after a downpour. Astonishing
contradiction, in fact, for it comes across austere and stan-
doffish and then comes over all soft, soppy, and instantly fruity
with eucalyptus, pine, grass and blackcurrant. Good partner
for roast food.

Cabernet/Merlot 1990 (Tesco)   13   £C

Timara Cabernet Sauvignon/Merlot 1990   12   £C

NEW ZEALAND WINE – *white*

Chardonnay (Tesco)   14   £C
Woody, rich and buttery in the mouth, although the fruit
seems to fight on the tongue. Great with chicken and rich fruit
dishes.

Dry White 12 £C
Attractive all-round wine with plenty of rounded fruit. Might be better, in fact, with less fruit and more of that searing New Zealand grassiness.

Jackson Estate Sauvignon Blanc 1992 15 £D
Typical grass cutting and celery nose, delicious balanced fruit (melons and distant echoes of lime zest). Beautiful finish. Lovely graceful wine of some class.

Sauvignon Blanc 1991 (Tesco) 13 £C
Spring flowers and cabbages.

Stoneleigh Chardonnay 1991 13 £D

Timara Chardonnay/Semillon 1992 13 £C

Villa Maria Chenin/Chardonnay 1991 13 £C

Villa Maria Sauvignon Blanc 1991 (half) 15 £B
This is deliciously bellicose: the tongue cowers in delighted shock, the taste buds quiver in agonized delight, and the throat gasps for another glass. If British tennis professionals took swigs of it between changes of ends, one of them might win Wimbledon.

PORTUGUESE WINE – *red*

Bairrada 1989 (Tesco) 13 £B
At under £3 it's being given away.

Borba 1989 15 £B
Dry with advanced rich fruit (figs and cherries), plummy overtones with a fondant chocolate finish. Superb! I have a

fondness for the town of Borba for it has fed me well on its broad bean and chorizo soup. I'm also partial to the bottling line of the wine co-operative which makes this wine, for it has the nerve to cheer the workers up with a quote, unmissably inscribed upon large ceramic tiles, from Europe's gloomiest writer after Franz Kafka, the Portuguese misanthrope Fernando Pessõa.

Dão 1989 (Tesco)   13   £B

Dom José   14   £A

This rural masterpiece of peasant pulchritrude has been likened to five-day-old lorry driver's socks, but the secret with this earthy fruit stew is to let it breathe for a bit before tackling it. Better, pour into a large earthenware vase (removing flowers first). It has been known to be specially promoted at £1.99 which is even more endearing.

Douro 1985 (Tesco)   13   £B

Periquita 1989   14   £A

Outstanding value for lots of good fruit.

Quinta da Cardiga   13   £B

Brilliant value.

Tinto da Anfora 1988   15   £C

Just yummy. Yummy smell, yummy taste, yummy to look at in the glass. Even the price tag's yummy (considering how many other yummies you're getting for your money). Drink it with roast beef and rich gravy and dine happy.

Tinto Velho 1986   14   £C

Soft leather, herbs and raspberries. Delightful.

PORTUGUESE WINE – *white and rosé*

Bairrada 1991 (Tesco)   14   £A
A plate of mussels in tomato sauce and a bottle of this wine
are perfect partners.

Cova da Ursa Chardonnay 1990   13   £D
Lemon on the pleasant fruity aroma, butter and almonds in
the mouth, some staying power to the finish. An unusual and
attractive chardonnay.

Dão 1991 (Tesco)   11   £B

Douro 1991 (Tesco)   11   £B
Sour fruit of interest but struggles to get fresh in the finish.

Dry Portuguese Rosé   12   £B

João Pires Moscato 1990   14   £C
No appetite? Take a glass of this.

SOUTH AFRICAN WINE – *red*

**Cabernet Sauvignon Coastal Region 1989
(Tesco)**   13   £C
Most attractive berried fruit, dry and well defined.

Cape Pinotage 1992 (Tesco)   13   £B
Excellent value pasta wine.

Meerlust Pinot Noir 1988   10   £E

Stellenbosch Merlot 1992 (Tesco)   13   £C

Zandvliet Shiraz 1987   11   £D
Typical sour-nosed dusty Aussie in feel (shiraz is an Aussie
grape after all) but less of the Aussie ring-a-ding fruit.

SOUTH AFRICAN WINE – *white*

Cape Chenin Blanc 1992 (Tesco)   14   £B
Apple and peardrop undertones to some excellent melon fruit.
Good fresh finish of some style. A wine to enjoy as an
end-of-the-workday solvent or to drink with complex salads
(e.g. tuna and tomatoes).

Cape Colombar, Robertson 1992 (Tesco)   14   £B
Delicious value. Attractive squashy, guava jam flavour, dry
undertones.

Chardonnay, Robertson 1992   14   £C
Delicious, full of fruit and balanced acidity. Good price, fine
style, excellently turned out product.

Danie de Wet Chardonnay 1991   13   £C

Fleur du Cap, Noble Late Harvest 1990 (50cl)   12   £C
Searingly sweet, treacle-tartish wine with not enough solid
botrytis (i.e. noble rot) complexity and concentration of fruit.
This is what that word 'noble' in the name means, referring as
it does to the technique of allowing grapes to rot on the vine
and to become infected with the botrytis fungus before
picking them, so that there is less water in the fruit and the
grape-sugars develop.

Goiya Kgeisje 1993   14   £B
A sauvignon blanc/chardonnay combination with a lovely

fruity backbone, excellent structure, and a considerable improvement on the '92 vintage which was solely sauvignon. The addition of chardonnay has filled out the wine yet kept masses of freshness and citric flavour and it is terrific fun drinking. It must be one of the first '93 vintage wines on sale. It also sports the most attractively original, and apposite, wine label I've seen in years, with perfectly weighted and designed typography and a superbly vibrant representation of an ostrich.

Oak Village Sauvignon Blanc 1992   13   £C
A very nicely turned out wine.

Swartland Sauvignon Blanc 1992 (Tesco)   12   £B
Curiosity, this, with its artichoke aroma. More like a chenin than a sauvignon.

Van Louveren Pinot Gris 1992   12   £C

SPANISH WINE – *red*

Don Darias   14   £B
It projects like a stage actor. Wonderful company.

Gran Don Darias   13   £B

Marqués de Chive   14   £B
Staggeringly good value for an oak-aged tempranillo (the rioja grape), this wine comes from the up and coming area west of Valencia called Utiel-Requena. Deliciously fruity (raspberry and plums), with a handsome touch of wood, and a firm finish. N.B. *Keep your meddling hands off the label, Tesco's design studio!* This is a cheapo bargain, *well* under three quid, and let's keep

it that way, and so can we hang on to the frumpy Spanish label, please? We don't want *expensive labels mucking up the price, thank you.*

Rioja Reserva 1985 (Tesco)	13	£D
Rioja (Tesco)	13	£C
Señorio de los Llanos 1987	14	£C
Toro 1989 (Tesco)	13	£C

Brilliant label! Like the wine, but love the label.

SPANISH WINE – *white*

Cinco Casas La Mancha 1992   14   £B
Delicious, slightly smoky, nicely edged, clean fruit. Well made. Excellent aperitif. Excellent value.

Don Darias   14   £B
With a spicy fish stew or curry, this is the wine.

La Mancha 1991   10   £B
Possibly what Sancho Panza used to swab down Rosinante.

Marqués de Chive   15   £B
Deep woody fruit. Very supple and rioja-like. Extremely cheap for the harmonious complexity of the style on offer here. A wine which will oil the wheels of a fish stew quite brilliantly.

Moscatel de Valencia (Tesco)   15   £B
Just over £3 makes this a honey of a bargain. And with it, your Christmas pudding goes down with a broad smile on its face.

Rioja (Tesco)	13	£C

Rueda 1991, International Winemaker Series 12 £B
Typical banana/peach/pineapple fruit.

Viña Amalia 1991	12	£B

Viña del Castillo 1991	12	£B

USA WINE – *red*

Californian Cabernet Sauvignon 14 £C
Tastes like a minor bordeaux with a touch of the sun. Excellent roast food wine.

Californian Red (Tesco) 13 £B
Interesting what went through the label designer's mind when (s)he designed this curious blue and somewhat incongruous townscape on the bottle. Maybe too much of this wine perhaps? Very audacious. The wine only surprises by being soft and dry and quiet-mannered.

Californian Zinfandel 13 £C
Quieter version of the rip-roaring spicy Californian; it surprises, and soothes, with its soft mannerisms.

Jack London Cabernet Sauvignon 1987 12 £F

USA WINE – *white*

Californian Chardonnay 13 £C
The Quiet American. Delicious restraint.

| Californian White (Tesco) | 12 | £C |

Chalk Hill Chardonnay 1990   13   £E
Interesting and inviting woodily perfumed aroma, velvety rich
fruit gracefully shaped by the acidity. Good structure to the
whole wine. Classy, but expensive.

Sebastiani Chardonnay   13   £C
Good value for money for this richness of fruit.

Wente Chardonnay 1989   13   £D

SPARKLING WINE/CHAMPAGNE

Asti Spumante (Tesco)   10   £C

Australian Sparkling Brut (Tesco)   15   £C
Lovely feathery feel and terrific fruit and acid balance making
it impressively elegant in the mouth. At under a fiver it is
outstanding value for money.

Blanc de Blancs Champagne (Tesco)   13   £G

Cava (Tesco)   13   £C
Good value under a fiver.

Champagne Premier Cru 1983 (Tesco)   11   £H

Champagne (Tesco)   13   £F

Chardonnay Frizzante   10   £B

Chardonnay Spumante   15   £D
Great value sparkler with a great touch of Italian bravura on
the typical chardonnay fruit.

Crémant de Bourgogne (Tesco) 13 £D

Crémant de Loire Rosé, Cave des Vignerons de Saumur 12 £D

Deutz, New Zealand 12 £F
Just like Deutz champagne from the well-known Rheims company.

Grand Duchess Brut Sparkling Wine, Russia 10 £C
Comradely, but only just.

Henri Mandois Champagne 12 £F

Lindauer Brut 12 £E
New Zealand's champagne copy.

Loridos Espumante 1987 11 £D

Louis Massing Grand Cru Blanc de Blancs 16 £E
Elegant, stylish and a great bargain. Properly mature. A special purchase this at a special price (and what a price!) and I cannot guarantee any will be on sale by publication date. However, there is the chance that Tesco might persuade the Massing family to release some more at the same price in time for Christmas and if they do I would like *Superplonk* readers to be the first to snap the wine up.

Michel Arnould Champagne 12 £G

Moscato d'Asti Gallo d'Oro 1991 13 £D
Peaches and pears tripping, without stumbling, on the tongue. Great with fresh fruit at the end of a meal.

Premier Cru Brut Champagne (Tesco) 14 £F
Classy, delicious and very well made. Knocks many a grand marque into a cocked hat.

Prosecco Spumante   12   £C
A Venetian curiosity: peaches and custard with bubbles. Good
starter.

Rosé Cava   12   £C

Salinger 1989   12   £E

Soave Classico Spumante   13   £D

Vintage Cava 1988 (Tesco)   13   £D
Attractive soft fruit but possibly not enough acidic personality
to successfully tickle champagne lovers' fancies.

Vouvray, Chevalier de Moncontour Brut   13   £D

Waitrose

We were having a midweek dinner at home, my wife and I, and the wine had the texture of crumbled velvet. Our two young children asleep, we were relishing the rare opportunity to linger over our food and savour each sip of the soft aromatic wine. My dearest remarked how marvellous it was I'd got out a special bottle. This was a special occasion, I retorted. My wife closed her eyes and sighed. I leaned across the table and poured more of the red wine into her glass. '£2.95 the bottle,' I whispered romantically, 'Waitrose.' And as my wife's jaw landed in her plate, I went off to get another bottle of Côtes du Ventoux Les Oliviers. Alas, not a bottle is left on the shelves, because Waitrose customers have drunk them all.

So even a woman living with a man professionally dedicated to the cause of cheap wine is taken aback upon discovering that the fabulous liquid in her glass comes from an absurdly inexpensive supermarket bottle. I can't blame her. I'm sometimes surprised myself at how little a terrific bottle costs. Take Waitrose's brandy from Jerez.

'There's been something,' I told *Weekend Guardian* readers last year, 'I've been meaning to get off my chest and into yours for a little while now.' This something was the brandy in question. Now brandy is not something I usually concern myself with. I cover fermentation, oddtimes fortification, but rarely distillation and if I did cover it I would not bother my taste buds over anything that emanated from Spain because brandy from that country tastes all the same to me: like the crucial ingredient in crème caramel. I opened Brandy de Jerez, therefore, with a good deal of suspicion and no great hopes. I am no tosspot where this sort of liquor is concerned but I must tell you that three large glasses had disappeared before I was satisfied that what had flowed across my tongue had not been an illusion but was as unctuously nutty (it is distilled sherry, after all) as I supposed. This brandy de Jerez is limpidly dry yet with a coyly fruity finish, like many a great oloroso, and it is superbly *different* in texture, class and style from any other Spanish brandy which has passed my lips. This heady experience, in spite of the punitive levels of duty such pleasures attract, is not marred by a weighty price ticket; the cost of this smoothly unaggressive 17-point brandy being £9.75 a bottle.

I should have guessed, stupid purblind me, that this brandy would be no slouch. For wasn't it a Waitrose bottle? And, curiously for this coy establishment, wasn't it prominently labelled as such? For some time now I've harboured suspicions that its booze-buying team, headed by Julian Brind Esquire, Master of Wine, is nigh unstoppable. Hardly a foot gets put wrong where quality and real individual buying flair are concerned and if one had only one shot at picking an outstanding wine off a supermarket shelf at midnight, blindfolded with the lights switched off, then Waitrose would be a good place to bring it off.

Of course, quite what this particular store thinks it is up to in putting such cheap marvels as that Côtes du Ventoux on its shelves is a mystery, for whenever I visit one of its stores it is overflowing with rich and famous customers who would, it seems to me, raise not an eyebrow at brandy asking fifty quid a bottle. Yet regularly they chug home in their walnut-fascia-ed limousines with terrific wines which cost £2.99 a throw.

Waitrose is the other end of the earth from Morrisons both spiritually and geographically. Indeed, if I write up a brilliant bargain at one of these stores in a *Guardian* article I always try to mention one or the other, aware that they attract two

species of customer who do not, cannot, and will never inter-
mix or marry even though they read the same newspaper of a
Saturday, so that in this way the great North/South divide, if
only for the brief moments it takes to read the *Superplonk*
column, is bridged.

Waitrose is as quintessentially southern English as
Brighton with its delightfully inhospitable pebbles and pawn-
shops; it's as Home Counties in style as strawberries at
Wimbledon, and the Pimms Tent at Henley. Any Japanese
tourist scheduled to visit Sainsbury or Tesco (for the reason
stated in this book's introduction) should bear this in mind.

The British Tourist Authority should inform foreign visi-
tors that at Waitrose there is more chance of meeting that
gracious, nearly extinct species, the mink-coated widow, than
at any other supermarket. Doubtless, because this canny crea-
ture picks up so many bargains at Waitrose she can still afford
the insurance for the coat.

AUSTRALIAN WINE – *red*

Brown Brothers Tarrango 1992   14   £C

It takes two to tarrango: the touriga grape of Portugal and a
sultana variety of white table grape called Thompson's seed-
less. There is much to recommend this marriage. The touriga, rich red in colour, tannin and flavour, offers a miserly
yield; the Thompson, on the other hand, is fecund to the point
of embarrassment. The marriage was arranged in Australia
and the resultant new grape makes for a deliciously fresh
wine, buzzing with young fruit and offering all the myriad
colours and flavours of summer pudding, and I would certainly rather drink it than a lot of Beaujolais – to which this

Tarrango, chilled and purply in the glass, rubbery and tingly-supple in the mouth, can be effortlessly compared. I would urge Tarrango upon anyone interested in the development of wine for it is a true talking point. If Brown Bros can get the price to below £3.50, it will become a major drinking point.

Château Reynella Stony Hill Shiraz 1989   15   £D
A big wine, dry yet overwhelmingly fruity, packed with complex flavours of plums, blackberries and blackcurrants all held together softly by a flavoursome woodiness. A bottle to satisfy a satyr.

Coldridge Estate Cabernet Sauvignon 1990   13   £C

Hardys Southern Creek Shiraz/Cabernet 1991   13   £B

Koonunga Hill Shiraz/Cabernet 1991   14   £C
One of the most consistently slurp-worthy under-a-fiver shiraz/cabernet marriages on sale.

Lachland Springs Cabernet/Shiraz 1991   15   £B
Bargain with a capital B and to cap that it's a Big Bruising Beaut of a bottle of wine. Has a herby, woody, blackcurranty aroma, oozes bouncing, brambly fruity and then offers a sweet fruit finish underlying the dry fruit feel. Succulent, smelly, swiggable.

Leasingham Domaine Shiraz 1989   13   £D
Smashing peppery stuff for barbecued foods.

Leasingham Domaine Shiraz 1990   14   £D

Lindemans Shiraz Bin 50 1990   14   £C
Typical brilliant Aussie value for money with lashings of delicious spicy fruit.

Peter Lehmann Cabernet Sauvignon 1990   14   £D
Damson, plum and apple to gargle, black cherry to swallow;
together they put a happy smile on anyone's lips. Also deliciously inviting aromatically. All round, extremely elegant
attire for an Aussie – the hat is silk and the corks dangling
from it are silver-plated.

AUSTRALIAN WINE – *white*

Currawong Creek Chardonnay 1991   14   £C
Meaty wine brimming with honeyed dry fruit. Delicious.

Hardys Nottage Hill Chardonnay 1992   15   £C
Rich, buttery aroma and flavour, yet clear and livening to
finish. One of the most pleasing chardonnays on sale under
£4.

Hardys Southern Creek Semillon/Chardonnay
1992   13   £B

Lachland Springs Semillon 1992   14   £B
With muscadet wanting and chablis pricey, here is the answer
for impecunious grilled fish and shellfish lovers: an extremely
demure Aussie with subtle lemon and melon hints along with
a clear, clean citric finish and a really daft price.

Mitchelton Reserve Marsanne 1990   15   £D
I've always been a fan of this wine and its not-exactly-world-
famous marsanne grape variety (which also grows in the
Rhône). The flavour of hot buttered hazelnuts on ogen melon.
Rich and delicious.

Mitchelton Sauvignon Blanc 1992   14   £C
Very Oz but also very not. You get the usual fruit but it's
unusually well polished and refined. Like an Etonian with an
Australian accent.

Oxford Landing Sauvignon Blanc 1992   14   £C
Delicious, green and fruity. Softer than a New Zealander of
this ilk. Brilliantly attractive wine.

Penfolds Koonunga Hill Chardonnay 1992   14   £C
Full lush fruit plus a ticklish dollop of lemon zest. Delicious,
but getting pricey near a fiver.

Simon Whitlam Chardonnay 1991   15   £E
Delicious wine with roast chicken or with a book. Rich in
flavour and style, yet sophisticated and well-mannered.
Lovely balance.

AUSTRIAN WINE – *white*

Grüner Veltliner 1991   14   £C
The aroma conjures up the image of an incarcerated librarian
with a wispy grey beard but then offers deliciously elegant
fruit which wouldn't be out of place experienced on the deck
of a luxury yacht idling at anchor in the Aegean.

BULGARIAN WINE – *red*

Bulgarian Country wine, Merlot/Pinot Noir   13   £B
Newly minted, these Bulgarian country wines seem rather

green and even a mite peppery but this character softens in
time and this wine is well on the way.

Cabernet Sauvignon Russe 1988   14   £B
Stupendous value: blackcurranty but gooey – gooey and rioja-
like. At this price who's grumbling?

Mavrud Assenovgrad 1988   13   £B

Merlot/Gamza   13   £B

CHILEAN WINE – *red*

Viña Carmen Cabernet Sauvignon 1989   13   £C
Blackcurrant fruit-pastille smell, good length to the fruit
which is very supple, quietly velvety and hinting at seriousness.

Concha y Toro Cabernet Sauvignon 1989   13   £C

CHILEAN WINE – *white*

Caliterra Chardonnay 1992   14   £C
Classy, stylish drinking. Subdued but delicious.

ENGLISH WINE – *white*

Hastings, Carr Taylor   14   £B
Fruit, acidity, perfume, structure, balance, price. It's got the
lot in the right proportions.

FRENCH WINE – *red*

**Baron Villeneuve du Château Cantemerle,
Haut-Médoc 1990**   13   £E
California style claret. Delicious stuff now, but velvet in five
years' time or so.

Beaujolais-Villages 1992   12   £C

Bourgogne Pinot Noir, Buxy 1990   11   £D

Brouilly 1992   12   £C

Cabernet Haut-Poitou 1990   12   £C
Cabernets franc and sauvignon combine to make a fried
sausage sizzle even more.

Cabernet Sauvignon, Vin de Pays d'Oc 1991   13   £C

Cahors Cuvée Reserve 1990   12   £B
Interesting chewy fruit, rather tasty with Greek food I fancy.

Château Bourdac 1989   12   £D

Château d'Agassac 1988, Loudon Haut-Médoc   13   £E

Château de Nages, Costières de Nîmes 1991   11   £B
Not yet in the class of the terrific 1990. Some woody intrigue

to the aroma, but the fruit is struggling to come through. Will improve in bottle.

Château de Prade, Côtes de Castillon 1989   13   £D
Smooth, aromatic, tasty, yet soft and mouth-crunchingly dry.

Château Grand-Puy-Lacoste 1987   14   £F
This could be kept to be drunk into the next century, but it offers depth and satisfaction now. With garlicky roast lamb and flageolet beans it is a wine sublime.

Château Marseau, Côtes du Marmandais 1990   12   £B

Château Peyre-Lebade, Listrac 1989   11   £E

Château Tour Martines 1990   13   £C
Put it down for a couple of years. It may well become a 15 pointer.

Châteauneuf-du-Pape 1990   13   £E

Châteauneuf-du-Pape, Comte de Lauze 1990   14   £E
Classic, touch drier than some but all the jaunty smoothness the style is famous for, with that little prickle of spice.

Chorey-les-Beaune, Domaine Maillard 1990   13   £E
Delicious aroma and flavour.

Claret, Patrice Calvet 1989   12   £C

Côtes de Duras 1990   12   £C

Côtes du Rhône 1991 (Waitrose)   13   £B
Dry, but sweet-fruit finishing. Cosy and slip-downable. A beginner's Côtes du Rhône.

Crozes-Hermitage Cave des Clairmonts 1990   12   £D

Cuvée Adelaide Corbières 1991   13   £C

Domaine de Beauséjour, Côtes la Malepère
1991   12 £B

Domaine de La Présidente   14 £B
Ugly republican name especially with that capital L, and it
also sports a large and lonely tree on its label into the trunk of
which some drunk has attempted to carve his initials AV but
missed. 'Vin de Pays de la Principauté d'Orange' the label
says (twice), obviously proud of its obscure and unsung appellation which lies in the no-man's-land between the Rhône and
Provence. But the cinsault, grenache and syrah (I guess)
grapes in the wine are well strung together, soft and earthy,
with a nice meaty edge with good acidic balance. In spite of a
label which can only attract incontinent canines, this wine will
bring cheer to any table.

Domaine de St-Macaire, Vin de Pays de
l'Hérault   11 £B

Domaine des Fontaines, Vin de Pays d'Oc 1991 16 £B
How it is that Waitrose customers haven't swallowed every
bottle of this '91 is baffling. Is the wine too cheap? The fruit
isn't as vibrant as it was a year ago but it's still one of the most
engaging merlots for the money I've ever tasted.

Domaine St-Germain Minervois 1990   13 £B

Gamay Haut-Poitou 1991   12 £C

Good Ordinary Claret Bordeaux (Waitrose)   13 £B
A bargain – also available in a magnum for six quid odd. It's as
good as its name and better than ordinary (thus offering us the
only understatement ever made by a supermarket own-label
bottle.)

Hautes Côtes de Beaune 1990   13 £D

Les Forts de Latour, Pauillac 1985   11   £H

Margaux 1990   13   £E
Lovely classic drinkable Margaux.

Médoc 1991   12   £C

Moncenay 1990   12   £C

Moulins de Citran Haut-Médoc 1989 (half)   13   £C
This is this book's first Japanese wine, for a Japanese company
owns the vineyard. This is utterly undetectable in the wine,
which is a proper claret with authentic (and subtle) touches of
dry cedary blackcurrant. Considering the way Japanese com-
panies invest long term, improve every year, and compete like
hell, this wine may well be on a par with Château Lafite by
2050 – though never this particular bottle.

Prieuré Fonclaire Buzet 1990   13   £C

St-Amour, Domaine du Carjot 1992 (half)   13   £B

St-Amour 1992, Les Poulets (half)   13   £B

St-Chinian   11   £B

St-Emilion   13   £D

St-Joseph, Caves de St-Desirat 1989   13   £D
Sexy wine with a cigar-like edge to the fruit. Rather unwilling
to cooperate with its fruit as forcefully as the previous vintage
but this reluctance may soften over the months ahead and, I
suspect, the wine will cheerfully turn out splendid in the end.

Saumur, Domaine du Moulin de l'Horizon 1990 13   £C
Earthy, dark cherry fruit, dry, attractive.

Savigny-les-Beaune Faiveley 1990   13   £E

Special Reserve Claret 1989 (Waitrose) 13 £C
Excellent value real claret: woody, blackcurranty, primly and properly dry.

**Syrah, Vin de Pays des Comtes Rhodaniens
1992** 13 £B

Vieux Château Gaubert Graves 1989 13 £D

Volnay 1988 10 £F
Authentic, ten-quid-plus, vegetal aroma but thereafter only a three-quid dollop of fruit rather than the nigh-on £13 the price sticker demands to take the bottle away.

Volnay Premier Cru 1988 10 £F

FRENCH WINE – *white and rosé*

Alsace Gewürztraminer 1990 14 £D
Delicious floral gem with subtle lychee fruit and a touch of spice. Not hugely concentrated but delicious.

Best de Bordeaux Tradition 1990 13 £D
Not the most winning name, but some winning fruit with creamy woody undertones. Excellent with grilled chicken.

Blanc de Mer 14 £B
Now also in a magnum, for under six quid, this is the wine for large gatherings of the British chapter of the Bouillabaisse Club.

Blaye Blanc 1992 13 £B
Pleasant pear-and-peach-drop fruit.

Bordeaux Blanc Medium Dry   11   £B

Bordeaux Sauvignon 1992   12   £B

Bourgogne Aligote Brocard 1992   12   £D

Cabernet Rosé Haut-Poitou 1992   13   £C

Chablis Gaec des Réugnis 1992   13   £D

Chablis Premier Cru, Mont de Milieu 1991   13   £E
Makes a decent stab at depth and class.

Chais Baumière Chardonnay 1991   15   £C
Lovely oil-rich chardonnay with melony fruit. Excellent value
under £4.

Chardonnay Haut-Poitou 1992   13   £C

**Château Bastor-Lamontagne Sauternes 1989
(half)**   15   £E
Huge, mouth-filling sauternes with the unctuousness and
liquid smoothness of a Disraeli. A pudding in itself.

Château Darzac 1992   13   £C

Château de Rochemorin 1990   15   £E
Continuing in the Lurton/Rochemorin tradition of gracious
whites this vintage has developed well over the past twelve-
month and has New World peardrop hints to the well-formed
Old-World fruitiness.

Château du Rival Bordeaux 1992   14   £C
Very pretty wine with a touch of woodiness to the firm, full,
freshly finished fruit.

Château Haut-Rian Bordeaux 1992   14   £C
Green and fresh with subtle melony fruit. Very attractive wine.

Château la Calevie Monbazillac 1990 16 £D

My favourite Monbazillac for the money. Rich butterscotch flavour and sweetness. Fantastic wine. Wonderful with blue cheese and a bunch of grapes.

Château Loupiac Gaudiet 1988 14 £D

A tasty lot of rot for the money.

Château Piada 1989 14 £G

I'd be a very happy bunny with a bottle of this wine, a fruity novel, a bunch of grapes, and a chunk of hard cheese for company.

Domaine de Hauret Lalande, Graves 1992 14 £C

Domaine Gibault, Sauvignon de Touraine 1992 16 £C

My neighbour, a much-travelled chap, thought the wine reminded him of sancerre. We were sitting on his front step, an eccentric undertaking in my part of central London in April, but nevertheless there we were drinking our way through a bottle of this very wine and I found myself nodding in agreement. Of course! The wine was exactly like some curious sancerre – gooseberryish, full of elegant greenage clean fruit with a lush soft edge to it, aromatic, delicious. Did I let on the wine cost under four quid? Well . . .

Domaine Petit Château Chardonnay, Vin de Pays du Jardin de la France 1992 15 £C

Lovely fresh style. Delicious, vibrant, citric-banana fruit with good balancing acidity.

Fortant Chardonnay, Vin de Pays d'Oc 1992 14 £C

A delicious level of rounded yet dryish fruit, properly finished off acidically.

Galliac Blanc 1992   14 £C
Lots of clear melony fruit and no complaints.

Haut-Poitou Sauvignon 1992   13 £C
Dry as a bone – and a green bone at that. Live oysters will
happily drown in it.

Jacquère, Vin de Savoie 1992   14 £C
Lovely tickle of grass and honey on the nose – classy, buttery
fruit – fine balance – a polite and gracefully mannered wine.

Mâcon Lugny Les Charmes 1991   13 £D

Meursault Les Grands Charrons 1990   10 £G
A lot of dosh, not a lot of posh.

Muscadet 1992 (Waitrose)   11 £B

Pinot Blanc d'Alsace Médaille d'Or 1991   14 £D
Very delicious, rich, apricot-finished fruit.

Pouilly-Fuissé 1991   13 £D

Pouilly-Fuissé, Les Chevrières 1990   11 £D

Pouilly-Fumé, Jean-Claude Châtelain 1992   12 £E

Premières Côtes de Bordeaux   13 £C
A pud wine. But the pud needs to be very light.

St-Veran 1992   13 £D

Sancerre 1992   12 £D

Sauvignon de St-Bris 1992   13 £D

Tokay Pinot Gris 1991   12 £D

Vilonds Muscat 1992   12 £C

Vin de Pays d'Oc Sur Lie 1991   13 £B

Vin de Pays de la Côte d'Or, Cépage Auxerrois 12 £C
Subtle toffee/honey touch to the aroma which carries
through to the fruit though this is a dry wine. If that sounds
odd and confusing, then rightly so, perhaps, for the grape
variety by the name of auxerrois can refer to the red grape,
also called malbec, which makes the deeply red wine of
Cahors, and it can also refer to a chardonnay-type grape
which does, naturally enough, make white wine but this is
the first instance, as far as I know, of its being vinified in
Burgundy. However, I may just be as confused as the grape
variety must be.

**Vin de Pays du Jardin de la France
Chardonnay**   13 £B
Pretty label – like Art Nouveau perfume. Surprise, surprise,
it smells like a muscadet but has good fruit and body. Good
value for fish barbecues.

Vouvray, Domaine de la Robinière 1992   12 £C

GERMAN WINE – *white*

Avelsbacher Hammerstein Riesling 1986   16 £E
Classic bottle of riesling. Touch youthful, perhaps, but oh
that riesling cut! Brilliant glittering acidity. Has enough zestiness and bite to arouse the dead. Not a wine for the faint-
hearted.

**Bad Bergzaberner Kloster Liebfrauenberg
Auslese 1992**   14 £C
A superb aperitif, with a glittering touch of honey.

Baden Dry   14 £B
Outstanding value for such vivid fruit, with a subtle touch of
ginger, and a good bottle for fish and chips.

Erben Kabinett 1991   13 £B
Delicious aperitif.

Erdener Treppchen Riesling Spätlese 1986   16 £D
Gorgeous zippy riesling wine. The aperitif wine of the year.
Or try with roast pork or oriental food, especially Thai.

Morio Muskat 1992   15 £B
Brilliant aperitif of great gooey, melony fruit without sweetness. Light (9.5% alcohol), cheap, and with decided personality.

Pinot Blanc Trocken 1990   14 £C
An excellent aperitif: good, nicely rounded fruit, with a dry
finish.

Riesling 1990 (Waitrose) (1 litre)   12 £C

GREEK WINE – *white*

Kouros Patras 1990   13 £C

ITALIAN WINE – *red*

Campo ai Sassi 1990   13 £D

Carafe Red Wine (Waitrose) (1 litre)   13 £C
Adds pizzazz to any pizza.

Chianti Classico Riserva, Rocca delle Macie
1990   13   £C

Grifi Avignonesi 1987   13   £F
Refined earthiness and softness.

Le Pergole Torte, Monte Vertine 1987   13   £G

Montepulciano d'Abruzzo 1990   15   £C
A lovely, swirlingly fruity wine as invigorating placed to the
lips after a day's slog as is an astringent put to the cheek after a
close shave.

Rosso Conero 1991   12   £C

Teroldego Rotaliano 1990   13   £C

ITALIAN WINE – *white*

Carafe White (Waitrose) (1 litre)   13   £C
Excellent value for a well-balanced dry white.

Chardonnay Alto Adige, Walch 1991   14   £C

Il Marzocco Chardonnay 1988   13   £F
It is stylish, clear and fresh, with an almost exotic Italian
spiciness to the typical chardonnay aroma and taste.

Orvieto Classico Cardeto 1992   13   £C

Santa Cristina Chardonnay, Zenato 1991   14   £D
Delicious, elegant, striking.

Soave Classico, Zenato 1991   13   £C
Very elegant, pretty, and thin, a delightful Kate Moss of a
wine.

Tocai di San Martino della Battaglia, Zenato
1990   13   £C

LEBANESE WINE – *red*

Château Musar 1986   16   £E
The Middle East's greatest wine without doubt. Gone up 50
per cent in price over the recent past but then the Bekaa
Valley is hardly the most congenial place to grow wine let
alone pick the grapes to make it. Musar is a fiery wine, a touch
theatrical perhaps, but it is warm and demanding of the
palate, and its role alongside richly stuffed poultry or game is
indisputably a great one. A wine to offer heroes, or the family
at a celebration lunch.

NEW ZEALAND WINE – *red*

Montana Cabernet Sauvignon 1991   13   £C

NEW ZEALAND WINE – *white*

Cooks Chardonnay 1991   12   £C

Jackson Estate Sauvignon Blanc Marlborough
1992   15   £D
The aroma is like one's first breath of clear spring ozone after

winter spent in polluted central London. Gooseberry-brilliant and fresh. Beautiful wine.

Villa Maria Sauvignon Blanc 1992   15   £C
Stimulating aroma of hay, slightly honeyed and gooseberryish. Full, ripe fruit, lushly formed. A most attractive bottle of pedigree sauvignon.

PORTUGUESE WINE – *red*

Bairrada Reserva Dom Ferraz 1989   13   £B
Soft plum fruit of some attractiveness, but not as excitingly boisterous a mouthful as previous vintages.

Pasmados 1986   14   £C
Touch of sweaty sock on the nose but handsome figgy fruit. Smashing pasta wine.

Tinto da Anfora 1989   13   £C
The '88, of which there may still be odd bottles around, offered a delightful sticky toffee and fig aroma, ripe rich fruit, and a wickedly silky finish – this '89 has to go some to be likewise considered.

SOUTH AFRICAN WINE – *red*

Fairview Estate Merlot 1990   13   £D
Delicious. Pricey but delicious.

Far Enough 1991   14   £B
Savoury, fruity, soft and inordinately gulpable. Terrific
bargain.

Stellenryck Cabernet Sauvignon 1987   13   £D

SOUTH AFRICAN WINE – *white*

Avontuur Chardonnay 1991   15   £C
Oily woody fruit but not oppressive since there's pure delight
in the lively balancing acidity which shrouds the wine in a
satiny cloak.

Robertson Sauvignon Blanc 1992   14   £B
Good value is beginning to pour out of South Africa and wine
drinkers are pouring it gratefully down their throats. This one
is no exception – except for a weedy finish (a small niggle in
an otherwise superb value-for-money tipple) it is an elegant
wine of excellent bouquet and mid-taste underpinned by a
pleasant fruit-drop tone to the fruity finish.

Sauvignon Blanc KWV 1992   12   £C

SPANISH WINE – *red*

Agramont Navarra 1989   14   £C
Touch of vanilla on the nose. Very attractive dry fruit.

Castillo de Liria Valencia   14   £B
An excellent mix of soft fruits at a bargain price.

Cosme Palacio Rioja 1989   14   £C
Rich, elegant rather than raffish. A lovely rioja of considerable style: dry, little ugly vanilla, very smooth.

Don Hugo   14   £B
Turns out regularly for Spain's first eleven, though finicky aficionados complain at its lack of finesse, but poured into a commonsense glass and held under a commonsense nose there is no grumbling at the lush aroma and evident fruitiness.

Ribera del Duero 1989   13   £C

Viña Alberdi Rioja 1988   13   £D

SPANISH WINE – *white and rosé*

Castilo de Liria Valencia (1.5 litres)   14   £D

Cosme Palacio Rioja 1990   12   £C

Don Hugo   15   £B
Full, creamy, banana-y, oaky, coconut-rich fruit yet not boiled or blowzy but surprisingly fresh and pleasant to roll across the molars. Perfect for watching flavourless food programmes on television but equally superb with paellas and fish curries.

Don Hugo Rosé   14   £B
An excellent value-for-money rosé with cherry and melon fruit.

USA WINE – *red*

Cartlidge & Browne Zinfadel 1990   14   £C
Zingy, zesty stuff which just flows down the throat and
screams with fruitiness all through the descent.

Fetzer Valley Oaks Cabernet 1990   14   £D
Very dry, meaty, full of mature fruit. A firm and true companion for roast dinners.

Robert Mondavi Pinot Noir, Napa Valley 1989   13   £E
Very, very attractive.

USA WINE – *white*

Bel Arbors 1992   15   £B
Absolutely scrumptiously attractive Californian plonk. Rich
fruit with vivid acidity underpinning it. Lovely wine.

St Andrew's Vineyard Chardonnay 1990   15   £E
Lovely fruit and wood integration. Elegant, fat, and taste-bud
hugging. Delightful wine.

St Andrew's Vineyard Chardonnay 1990   12   £E

SPARKLING WINE/CHAMPAGNE

Ana de Cordoníu Chardonnay 1989 (Spain)   16   £E
Stunning sparkler of great character: complete, full, elegant,
classy.

Angas Brut Rosé, Australian 14 £C
One of those Antipodean sparklers which deliciously tickle the nose and only lightly tickle the pocket but send shivers up the spine of champagne makers.

Blanquette de Limoux (Waitrose) 13 £D
Very attractive.

Cava Cristal Brut Castellblanch, Spain 12 £D

Champagne Brut Blanc de Noirs (Waitrose) 14 £F
Lovely big wine bubbling over with rich fruit.

Champagne Rosé (Waitrose) 15 £F
The closest the poor teetotaller can come to grasping the flavour of this scrumptious article is by chewing a digestive biscuit spread thickly with crushed rose petals and drinking Perrier water with a microscopically thin slice of lime zest.

Champagne Extra Dry 1986 (Waitrose) 14 £G

Champagne (Waitrose) 14 £F
One of the best supermarket champagnes you can buy.

Clairette de Die Tradition 1990 14 £D
An absolute peach of an aperitif.

Crémant de Bourgogne, Lugny 14 £D
Excellent dry (yet fruitily rounded) sparkling wine to be preferred to many, many champagnes.

Crémant de Bourgogne Rosé 13 £D

Green Point Vineyards Brut 1989, Australia 13 £E
Delicious, and exactly like a decent champagne but not a great one.

Le Baron de Beaumont Chardonnay   14   £D
Excellent value for a delightful little sparkler.

Liebfraumilch (Waitrose)   13   £C

Moscato d'Asti 1992   15   £C
Something to amuse your guests at the end of a meal or your
palate at the start. Sweet and honeyed, yes, but never cloying
and with that sparkle it has a fruity lightness of touch which
defies description (oh, all right, it's like picking up a peach
with a feather).

Santi Chardonnay Brut, Italy   14   £D
Delicious and cheap.

Saumur (Waitrose)   14   £D
Chewy little number of some distinction.

Seppelt Great Western Brut, Australia   16   £C
Superb bargain. A finer fizzer on sale for under a fiver it's
difficult to name. Lemony, zingy, zesty. Great style.

Rating guide

10, 11   Nothing nasty but equally nothing worth shouting from the rooftops. Drinkable.

12, 13   Above average, interestingly made. A bargain taste.

14, 15, 16   This is the exceptional stuff, from the very good to the brilliant.

17, 18   Really great wine, worthy of individual acclaim. The sort of wine you can decant and serve to ignorant snobs who'll think it famous even when it is no such thing.

19, 20   Overwhelmingly marvellous. Wine which cannot be faulted, providing an experience never to be forgotten.

PRICE BANDS

A Under £2.50	E £7.00–£10.00
B £2.50–£3.50	F £10.00–£13.00
C £3.50–£5.00	G £13.00–£20.00
D £5.00–£7.00	H Over £20.00